TEACHING GYMNASTICS

TEACHING GYMNASTICS

E. Mauldon
D.A.S.E., M.A.
*Formerly Deputy Principal, Lady Mabel College of
Education, Rotherham, Yorkshire.*

J. Layson
D.A.S.E., M.Ed.
*Director of Dance, University of Surrey,
formerly Lecturer, Department of
Physical Education, University of Leeds.*

Longman

London and New York

Pearson Education Limited
Edinburgh Gate, Harlow,
Essex CM20 2JE, England
and Associated Companies throughout the world.

*Published in the United States of America
by Addison Wesley Longman Inc., New York*

First published 1965
Second edition 1979
Second impression 1996
Reprinted by Longman Group UK Ltd. 1989, 1990, 1992 and 1999

ISBN 0-582-02950-3

Transferred to digital print on demand, 2002
Printed & Bound by Antony Rowe Ltd, Eastbourne

Preface

This book is intended to help all those interested in teaching gymnastics not only the specialist in the Secondary school but also the Middle and Primary school teacher whose responsibility is perhaps the greater.

Since teaching cannot be learned from a book, if this text is to be of value it must be used practically and adapted to the needs of individual classes. The suggestions are intended as possible starting points and it should be realised that this is not the only way to teach gymnastics. The successful teacher finds his own method of presenting material through a process of experimentation and using his accumulated experience to advantage.

Help is given in the organisation and division of a lesson, including general teaching points which must be considered if the material is to be of any value. Chapters 5 − 15 are subdivided under the following headings:

(a) *material*, where the development of specific themes is discussed so as to provide teachers with information as to what these constitute as well as ideas as to how particular themes are related;

(b) *teaching*, based on practical experience and concerned with appropriate styles and strategies for implementing such material in the gymnastic lesson;

(c) *apparatus*, where the principles of selection and arrangement are discussed and suggestions put forward for provision relative to the theme. It is hoped that these will lead teachers to consider the arrangement of apparatus and the wording of tasks thoughtfully and imaginatively. A key to the illustrated apparatus will be found on page vii.

Material has been separated from *teaching* as it is necessary for the teacher to have both depth and breadth of knowledge, only some of which may be passed on to the children. He must see the subject as a whole, whereas the children will be concerned mainly with their present experience. It is for the teacher to understand the correlation between themes and help his class to relate past and present work.

Under *teaching* and *apparatus* specific reference has been made wherever practical to work considered suitable for Junior, Middle or Secondary children. This has not been done consistently since in certain situations it is applicable to all three.

The decision whether or not to use photographs in a book dealing with movement is a difficult one to make. It is admitted that photographs are of limited value but they are included in those chapters where it is thought they augment or illustrate teaching points within the text.

It is also difficult to describe precisely the varied actions which might result from any given challenge. Therefore it has often been necessary to restrict examples to named skills such as handstands and cartwheels. This has certain disadvantages but such skills are given only as recognisable solutions to particular tasks and variations will no doubt arise as a result of inventive exploration.

One complete chapter is devoted to movement observacation as applied to gymnastics since this is undoubtedly an essential pedagogical tool if teachers are to assess what is needed and develop what is produced.

Finally a scheme of work is outlined which may be of use as a guide for teaching children between the ages of seven and thirteen or fourteen. It can only be a guide as the teacher alone knows the children and the circumstances.

The second edition includes two new introductory chapters which respectively place the teaching of gymnastics within an historical context and look at the educational relevance of gymnastics within the school curriculum.

March 1979   E.M.
                                                               J.L.

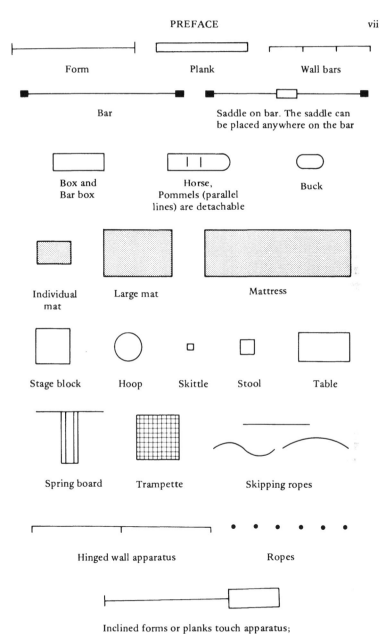

Form

Plank

Wall bars

Bar

Saddle on bar. The saddle can
be placed anywhere on the bar

Box and
Bar box

Horse,
Pommels (parallel
lines) are detachable

Buck

Individual
mat

Large mat

Mattress

Stage block

Hoop

Skittle

Stool

Table

Spring board

Trampette

Skipping ropes

Hinged wall apparatus

Ropes

Inclined forms or planks touch apparatus;
e.g. inclined form to bar box

Key to symbols used for apparatus illustrated in the text. With
minor exceptions the scale employed is 5 mm ≡ 480 mm.

Acknowledgments

Since we have retained certain photographs from the first edition we wish to repeat our thanks to Miss Hutton, Mr. Allen and Miss Crabbe, C.B.E., and to the two photographers Mr. Ian Sime and Mr. Don Holstead.

In the process of preparing this edition it was considered necessary to include a number of new photographs and we wish to record our gratitude to Mr. Stubbs, Headmaster of Wickersley Primary School, Rotherham, for his enthusiastic and helpful co-operation in making his pupils available for this purpose. We also found a ready response to our request for assistance from Mr. Mathews, Headmaster of Wickersley Comprehensive School and Mrs. T. Plowman and Mrs. C. Sayles, Head of the P.E. Department and member of the Physical Education staff respectively. In addition we would like to record our appreciation of the patience and expertise of Mr. Eric Daniels of the University of Leeds Photographic Department who took the new photographs.

Finally our thanks are due to the many friends and colleagues who gave generously of their time to read, discuss and correct the original text and to others who over the intervening years have offered constructive criticisms, some of which have resulted in modifications to the text of this edition.

E.M.
J.L.

Contents

CHAPTER 1

Historical Overview

The history of the development of what over the years has been variously termed educational gymnastics, modern educational gymnastics, basic movement, inventive movement, movement, movement education, movement training and so on, has yet to be written in detail. Indeed even its beginnings are obscure since it seems difficult to set a time when and a place where this type of gymnastics can be said to have become an identifiable form. However, there is little doubt that educational gymnastics evolved partly as a reaction against what was seen as the rigidity of Swedish and Austrian gymnastics and partly as a response to a changing educational climate in which notions such as "creativity" were becoming central. If the above two factors were instrumental in causing some physical educationists to reassess the nature and the place of gymnastics in education, then it was the work of the movement theorist Rudolf Laban (1879–1958) which enabled the protagonists of the new gymnastics to develop its theoretical framework.

Therefore, in the absence of a complete historical study of educational gymnastics, it would seem profitable to attempt to outline the main stages in its development in order to place the two editions of this book within a context. One immediate way in which this might be carried out would be by reference to all the major publications on educational gymnastics, however, in this chapter the source material is confined almost entirely to text books since the many articles in the various professional journals would require a more exhaustive study than the present overview permits. Nevertheless, reference to the major text books in chronological order does show, in a quite striking manner, the ways in which both the content of educational gymnastics and the methods of teaching it have developed and clarified over the years.

Webb (1967), in her work on the training of women teachers of physical education from 1800 to 1966, cites evidence, such as timetables and syllabuses, to show when the various colleges introduced educational gymnastics, for example, at I.M. Marsh College, Liverpool, the innovation occurred during the 1945—46 period. The Ministry of Education (now the Department of Education and Science) publications *Moving and Growing* and *Planning the Programme* (published in 1952 and 1953 respectively) exemplify the thinking of some leading physical educationists at this time. Both books are concerned with physical education in the primary school, of which gymnastics is seen as a part, and the influence of a child-centred, creative movement approach to the work is evident. However, although these publications were intended to replace the 1933 Syllabus of Physical Training for Schools and the new movement orientated basis for gymnastics is made explicit, the actual material of gymnastics is as yet relatively unstructured. Thus, while a qualitative movement approach is advocated, the lesson is planned as in Swedish gymnastics with the stress on developing mobility and strength by progressively working through parts of the body. An example given of a gymnastic activity is the mobilising of the arm and shoulder girdle through swinging actions that might be performed on a bar quickly or slowly, with twisting and in different directions.

The first text book on educational gymnastics was written by Morison (1956) and whereas in the Ministry of Education publications Laban's motion factors and elements are described but not acknowledged Morison both refers to and uses Laban's movement principles to provide the framework for her gymnastic material. In this book the nature and content of gymnastics, particularly as distinct from modern educational dance, becomes established, as is the method of teaching and learning. The former is by a series of progressive challenges, with both action tasks and movement tasks described, and the latter by exploration and experiment with no pre-determined hierarchical skill structure.

In the second of her two earlier books Morison (1960) retains the Laban basis but a thematic division of material becomes evident. The gymnastic themes which subsequent authors have used as the main method of structuring gymnastic material are all mentioned by Morison, some such as flight and balance, are dealt with in detail, others such as twisting and turning, symmetry and asymmetry are given less space. In these text books, therefore, Morison established the basis upon which educational gymnastics developed.

However, during this period of innovation educational gymnastics was not evolving along one clearly discernible line as instanced by Randall's 1961 publication *Basic Movement. A New Approach to Gymnastics.* The appearance of the term "basic movement" reflects ideas current at this time, for while Randall uses it virtually as a synonym for gymnastics others consider it as a form of movement training not specifically gymnastic, but giving a movement experience which is both basic and relevant to other physical education activities. Randall bases her text on what she terms Laban's "movement qualities", nevertheless she takes issue with Morison's interpretation of the flow factor as applied to gymnastics. Morison (1956) claims that gymnastics "produces very little truly flowing movement" but Randall argues that both free and bound flow are present in gymnastics and that flow "might be called continuity of movement." Another area of dispute evident from the inception of educational gymnastics was the seemingly ever-widening gulf between the types of gymnastics advocated by the men's and women's specialist colleges of physical education. This is reflected in Randall's assertion that "masculine and feminine gymastics have, to a great extent, essentially different aims and objectives."

An example of the criticisms levelled at educational gymnastics in the mid-fifties and early sixties by an eminent physical educationist not involved with its development can be found in Munrow's *Pure and Applied Gymnastics.* The first edition, published in 1955, was already questioning the nature of a gymnastic training which appeared to disregard mobility, strength and endurance. Randall (1961) attempted to counter some of Munrow's points but by the time Munrow wrote his second edition in 1963, he had at his disposal the three publications of Morison (1956, 1960) and Randall (1961) and his criticisms of educational gymnastics therefore become much more specific.   In particular he queried not only the claims made for the work but also the relation of the content of an educational gymnastic lesson to such claims.

Nevertheless, from the early sixties onwards the number of text books published on educational gymnastics showed a marked increase. The rapidly growing status of this form of gymnastics can be judged by the fact that the next public-action was by the then London County Council in 1962. Entitled *Educational Gymnastics. A guide for Teachers*, it was based on material used at the L.C.C.'s numerous in-service courses. The format follows that of Morison's books, since Laban's motion factors are explained briefly, and the teaching material is arranged under the headings of themes.   An interesting feature is that the lesson plan still shows the influence of more formal work for it is advocated that teachers should divide the floorwork into tasks related to the whole body, to weight "supported on the arms" and to "leg work".

The Bilbrough and Jones (1963) book, *Physical Education in the Primary School*, which covers a range of physical activities in the primary school, gives a physical education context to educational gymnastics and this, together with that of Cameron and Pleasance (1963) which has a title variation of *School Gymnastics*, are typical examples of the stage of development reached in educational gymnastics by this time. The material is now clearly defined, though relatively little detail is given, but there are many suggestions and ideas for the teacher to incorporate into lessons. The manner of teaching outlined is one where the open-ended problem solving situation is interspersed with more specific challenges in which the objective is to produce a recognisable skill or to give a particular movement experience.

In 1965 no less than four books on educational gymnastics were published. Both the I.L.E.A. (formerly the L.C.C.) and the Cameron and Pleasance books appeared in second editions, an indication of a continuing demand, and the latter in its revised form contained an appendix in which thirteen lesson themes were set out in response to requests from teachers. Pallett's (1965) *Modern Educational Gymnastics* uses the term preferred by many teachers since it acknowledges the relationship between educational gymnastics and modern educational dance and their common source in the work of Laban. It is also interesting in that it claims to help teachers trained in Ling's Swedish Gymnastics to adapt to the newer thematically structured educational gymnastics. The final chapter on "Poise" is significant too, since the responsibility of the physical education teacher for undertaking remedial work in the gymnastic lesson had by this time been discarded by most advocates of educational gymnastics.

The first edition of *Teaching Gymnastics* was also published in 1965. To the authors it seemed that despite the growing number of publications it was necessary to help teachers to distinguish between the preparation and presentation of gymnastic material, hence the format of dividing each theme into material, teaching and apparatus. In addition to the chapters devoted to specific themes, other chapters such as "Lesson Plan and Organisation", "Movement Observation" and "Syllabus and Progressions" were included in order to provide teachers with an appropriate pedagogical framework. In retrospect it is interesting to refer to some of the points made in the first edition of *Teaching Gymnastics* since much that was predicted in 1965 has become fact in the late 1970s. For example, the suggestions that when the gymnastic potential of Junior school children is realised it would be possible for them to tackle the so-called "advanced" themes and that educational gymnastics in the middle of the Secondary school should become an optional activity are now both generally accepted. Another feature of *Teaching Gymnastics* was the explicit statement of teaching aims, subsequently much quoted, and in the light of recent developments the twin aims of skill and understanding are of significance.

In 1966 the I.L.E.A. published a further teaching guide, *Movement Education for Infants* in which the Laban based thematic gymnastic material is given under "Movement Training" and "Agility" as part of a wider movement education. In the following year Cope's *Discovery Methods in Physical Education* appeared, reflecting new approaches to learning, and in 1969 four more gymnastic text books were published each with its particular style and emphasis. Of these four Morison's *A Movement Approach to Educational Gymnastics* is probably the most important. This book, published thirteen years after her first statements on the subject, constitutes a detailed and thoroughly worked out exposition on educational gymnastics. The material of her first two books is completely revised and much that is new added. However, the main feature of this book and the one that distinguishes it from all other text books on educational gymnastics is the style in which it is written. The descriptive language and the use of words that recapture the kinesthetic experience of gymnastics imbue the text with a characteristic flavour which probably stems from Morison's own concern and emphasis for the qualitative elements of skill.

Of the three other 1969 publications Allen's book, although orthodox in its explanation of Laban's theories as applied to gymnastics and based on the now common thematic structure, was written primarily for the New Zealand market, for by this time educational gymnastics, under various titles, was being taught in Australia, Canada and other countries. Buckland's book, simply entitled *Gymnastics*, is part of the "Activity in the Primary School" series and whereas earlier text books for this age group tended to cover the whole spectrum of physical education with educational gymnastics as an integral part, Buckland writes solely on gymnastics, perhaps an indication of the growing awareness of the particular relevance of this activity for Primary/Middle school children. The Cameron and Cameron publication *Education in Movement in the Infant School* begins with the familiar analysis of movement based on Laban's work and is followed by a chapter enumerating the various gymnastic themes. However, as with many other authors, only three of Laban's motion factors, that is time, weight and space are referred to for it appears that the flow factor is the one aspect with which advocates of educational gymnastics have had difficulty in relation to the development of themes. This problem can be traced back through the text book literature to Randall's (1961) criticism of Morison's (1956) interpretation of flow as applied to gymnastics.

Anderson's *Inventive Movement* published in 1970 is yet another text book written for Primary school teachers, and its title reflects the attitudes of some physical educationists who wish to distinguish between the notions of inventiveness and creativity and therefore prefer the terms inventive movement and creative movement to those of educational gymnastics and modern educational dance.

In 1972 there were two government publications on physical education which included sections on gymnastics. *Movement: Physical Education in the Primary Years* was published by the D.E.S. and is important insofar as it is the successor to *Moving and Growing* (1952) and *Planning the Programme* (1953). Its format is similar to the earlier publications, that is, a first part concerned with movement generally and a second part devoted to particular physical education activities, but the contents are more specific probably reflecting the development of the work during the intervening years. The influence of Laban is acknowledged and a brief summary of the main tenets of his theories given. The section on gymnastics (the term is not qualified by "educational") is presented under headings which approximate to the themes of the standard texts, along with numerous action photographs. The book is descriptive rather than prescriptive and the intention is to aid non-specialist teachers with an emphasis on "the application of general education principles and an understanding of movement in the physical education programme." The other 1972 publication is by the Scottish Education Department, titled *Physical Education in Secondary Schools. Curriculum Paper 12*. In some respects it is complementary to the D.E.S. publication since it focusses upon Secondary schools and is written in the form of a summary of the deliberations of a working party together with that group's recommendations; the overall impression is again one in which teachers are encouraged to select and pursue certain curriculum material and teaching strategies rather than being given set syllabuses.

Official statements apart, however, publication of text books on educational gymnastics has continued in the 1970s at a steady rate. Holbrook's (1973) *Gymnastics* follows the trend of being written specifically for the teacher of the five to eleven age group, is Laban based and thematically structured. Brigg's (1974) *Movement Education* is reminiscent of Randall's (1961) book, for not only is the term "basic movement" used but also a chapter entitled "Basic Movement into Educational Gymnastics" is included. The section on gymnastics is set out in the form of a series of progressive lessons based on thematically akin material. Two other aspects are worth noting, firstly, the gymnastics glossary in which many terms associated with more formal gymnastic systems appear, such as screw vault and longfly, and secondly, the suggestions for new apparatus such as "body bouncers" and "tiger stools", ideas again similar to those of Randall's "life belt" and "split horse with swivel pommels".

Williams' (1974) *Themes for Educational Gymnastics* has an explicit thematic structure with an implicit Laban influence. The book is specifically orientated towards the student teacher and the young teacher and therefore concentrates on providing reference material within a given gymnastic and educational framework. The brief but nevertheless significant section (developed more fully in a later paper, 1978) on "concept of self", with the sub concepts of "body image", "body concept" and "body schema" indicates how the "body awareness" notion of the 1940s and 1950s, always very generalised and never rigorously examined, is being considered anew with research underlining its relevance and importance to a system of gymnastics which claims a place in the school curriculum.

It is pertinent at this point in the tracing of the development of educational gymnastics to refer to a paper by Lewis (1978). This departure from what is otherwise an historical overview of text books is justified on the grounds that Lewis' paper pinpoints two crucial areas in educational gymnastics, the first, that of body concept, continues the discussion initiated by Williams and the second, that of gymnastic themes, departs from Williams and most other authors in the area. Lewis suggests that a "workable body concept" is that of "body integrity" and develops her argument into a proposal that educational gymnastics offers one of the richest ranges of bodily experiences to children. It would seem, therefore, that in the future this justificatory aspect of educational gymnastics will be one in which much interest will be shown and multi-disciplinary research undertaken. In the second part of her paper Lewis criticises what she sees as the stultifying effect on gymnastic work of adherence to a strict thematic approach. This possibility was anticipated by Morison who advocated "composite themes" but Lewis asserts that Morison's notion is "rarely put into action". Therefore, Lewis offers an alternative structure to what she terms "traditional themes" in the form of "action phrases". An action phrase such as "rise, spread and turn" would be adopted as the topic for a gymnastic lesson rather than a theme, since it is claimed that, unlike the latter, an action phrase contains several movement aspects and it could therefore be carried through the lesson in floor, partner and apparatus work without the class becoming bored and the gymnastic actions stereotyped. Lewis's criticism of the thematic approach may be true *per se;* it may be, however, that what is at issue stems more from unimaginative teaching than the manner in which the gymnastic material is organised. Perhaps this might also become a topic for future debate.

The publication of *Movement in Practice* by Learmouth and Whitaker (1976) is particularly interesting when examined within an historical context since it has some aspects which link it to the beginnings of educational gymnastics and others which place it very much in the second half of the 1970s. Despite the title, the term "educational gymnastics" is used throughout the text although the authors state that the work could equally well be described as "movement" or "movement training". The interchange-ability of terms is reminiscent of the mid 1940s to early 1960s period when the terminological debate was current. The main part of the book is concerned with fourteen series of progressive lessons, each series based on a specific theme, but an appendix, "Formative and corrective movement", echoes some of the characteristics of earlier gymnastic systems. While Learmouth and Whitaker are clearly not justifying educational gymnastics on remedial grounds their advocacy of the prevention of physical defects by the regular inclusion of formative and corrective movement in lessons is, in some senses at least, an extrinsic claim for educational gymnastics as distinct from the intrinsic claims relating to concepts of "self" and "body integrity" proposed by Williams and Lewis.

There are two features of the Learmouth and Whitaker

book which are characteristic of educational gymnastics in the late 1970s. The first of these is the influence of Olympic gymnastics which can be seen clearly in the many photographs which illustrate their text. It is probably inevitable that the previous clear dividing line between Olympic and educational gymnastics should have become blurred over time and while it would be an interesting study to assess the degree to which each system has influenced the other it is beyond the scope of the present historical overview to do so. However, it is sufficient to note that the coverage of Olympic gymnastics by television and the press as well as the B.A.G.A. awards have both had an effect on the recent development of educational gymnastics. Similarly, a perusal of such Olympic gymnastic texts as Allison (1963), Stuart (1964) and Prestidge (1972) indicate the way in which modern teaching methods and ideas have affected this form of gymnastics and it is therefore not surprising to read that Prestidge (1972) cites "body awareness" as an essential quality of a gymnast. The second contemporary feature of the Learmouth and Whitaker book is the mention of an aesthetic aspect to educational gymnastics. The comparatively recent interest in aesthetics may derive in part from the current debate on the nature and place of physical education in the curriculum and the not inconsiderable visual impact of Olympic gymnastics on television.

1979 brings the second edition of *Teaching Gymnastics* which, while omitting specific reference to Laban but retaining the thematic structure, also reflects current issues, and, like the first edition, attempts to predict future developments in gymnastics. The inclusion of two new chapters is an acknowledgment of the need to place gymnastics within its historical framework and educational setting.

The dual aims as stated in 1965 have been extended to three, *skill* and *understanding* are augmented by the inclusion of *appreciation* which although mentioned in the original edition was then linked to understanding. In this second edition, however, appreciation incorporates an aesthetic dimension which has wider educational implications.

The references to biomechanical aspects of certain gymnastic actions are made in the authors' belief that the more knowledge and understanding the teacher has of all relevant movement material the better equipped he is to teach the subject. This inclusion is prompted too by the fact that a growing number of physical educationists are considering the subject within the wider context of the interdisciplinary study of human movement. Some of the new photographs in the second edition are of children who have had varying degrees of experience in Olympic gymnastics either at school or in a club and these are included not only because they illustrate points made in the text particularly well but also because the authors acknowledge the cross influences between the two forms of gymnastics.

In summarising the historical development of educational gymnastics as derived from the major text books it could be said that the 1940s and 1950s period was one of innovation, in the 1960s the material and the method were clarified and consolidated and in the 1970s the emphasis has been theoretically and conceptually orientated.

The question of whether gymnastics survives as a subject worthy of curriculum space in the 1980s may hinge on several factors and under the pressures of demands for "relevance" its educational viability may well need to be further clarified and made more explicit than in the past.

CHAPTER 2

Gymnastics in the Curriculum

There is no doubt that education is becoming increasingly associated not only with talk of teacher accountability, in terms of the measurement and assessment of achievement against established standards of pupil performance, but also whether such achievements can be seen to serve the changing needs of children and society.

This fact, together with the possible emergence of a centralised core curriculum, seems to indicate an urgent need for teachers to reconsider current practice in physical education and be able to justify what they are teaching on grounds which both satisfy themselves and those asking the questions and making the decisions.

This chapter is an attempt to look critically at what could be said to constitute present claims for the retention of gymnastics within the physical education curriculum (assuming this in itself can be justified) and to put forward a case for certain alternative views.

That gymnastics has been regarded as educational in the past is self evident since it has for many years enjoyed a central position within the physical education programme and has managed to maintain this place in one form or another for well over half a century. One reason for this may be that it has been sufficiently flexible in its content to respond to the changing needs and demands of society at large whether these have been to do with health, fitness, disciplined response, harmonious development of mind and body or, more recently, aesthetic considerations.

There may also be more specific reasons for its uncritical acceptance since, at least in the Primary school, many view gymnastics as originating in children's *"natural"* activities such as running, swinging, climbing, hanging, rolling, inverting and so on and bringing the "natural" environment within the range of all children, albeit in a simulated and artificial manner. Indeed gymnastic feats do seem to be more readily associated with "skill hungry" young children who are physically highly active and tend to seek sensations concomitant with balance, loss of balance, inversion, flight and fall; all new and exciting experiences tinged with danger of a kind — of "voluptuous panic" to quote Callois.

But this claim can be called into question on two counts; firstly it could be argued that gymnastic activities are, in one sense, far from "natural" in that the upright stance as distinct from inversion, for example, is normally associated with human beings, and secondly that even if this were the case why should something considered "natural" automatically be thought educationally worthy of development? There are those who would argue that most children left to their own devices would adequately satisfy their physical needs and that there is therefore little if any need in an already over-crowded timetable to include such activities in the curriculum, rather the time should be reallocated to those areas of learning which are deemed at least as important and worthwhile but which most children do not turn to naturally, for example, reading and computation.

Some teachers may also claim that children find gymnas-tics *enjoyable* but like the previous point this is insufficient justification since there are many activities children would enjoy that are excluded from the curriculum on other grounds and there are other activities which may not initially be enjoyable but which for "educational" reasons are included on the timetable. And so although enjoyment may well be a powerful and necessary motivating factor in any learning situation it cannot count as a sufficiently good argument for including gymnastics in schools.

Yet another reason perhaps why it has remained firmly embedded within the curriculum is that it has claimed to provide opportunities for children not only to acquire specific neuro-muscular skills but also to be initiated into certain *social* mores, such as sharing, learning to lead and to follow as well as participating in the give and take of group situa-tions. It must be assumed, however, that such qualities are thought to be transferable and since the whole question of direct transfer is highly debatable the value of such a claim is somewhat undermined.

Its survival might also be explained in that the very use of the term *educational* gymnastics implies its value as a curriculum subject. But the fact must be faced that merely to label a subject "educational" by no means ensures that the subject itself is worthy of the title, neither does it necessarily follow that because a subject is taught using a method accepted as "educational" its content merits time-table time. In other words the means does not automatically justify the end.

There is, however, a whole new area of research which seems to be providing evidence of the relatedness of motor development, cognitive development and concept formation which may well be of direct relevance to the question under discussion and indicate a possible re-orientation of gymnastics at least in the Primary and Middle school. Rousseau, Dewey and Piaget, for example, have all indicated the ways in which children learn by functionally interacting with the environment and it is now generally accepted that the physical exploration of space, for example, becomes the foundation on which the conceptual idea of space is later built. A space concept is made up of constructs about one's own body as space, objects as space and spatial interrelationships, just as the child is able to develop the more difficult concept of time because he does things in time and things happen to him in time. More recently the importance of the body image has been recognised as a necessary stage in the acquisition of the self concept; a point that has been made in relation to gymnastics by Williams (1974, 1978) and which is referred to by Lewis (1978) within the notion of "body integrity." Brooke and Whiting (1973) and others have amassed a considerable amount of evidence to support the theory that movement experiences including those of a gymnastic-like nature, are crucial if development as a whole is not to be impaired. Material, therefore, in the form of literature and research findings which are now available needs to be studied and areas of physical education, including gymnastics, reviewed in the light of these findings. Not only should the most relevant and appropriate experiences be defined but also the way these can best be structured so as to be most effective. It may well be that by providing different shapes for children to manoeuvre, different surfaces to work on, varying distances and heights for them to master, we are already satisfying their needs in this respect, but to date there is no procedure for assessing what development is taking place or what progress is being made. Teachers and students more fully aware of the relationships between particular activities and the formation of specific concepts would surely be better able to structure situations which might have a greater chance of achieving the desired end.

Maybe a valid case could then be made for the inclusion of gymnastic activity within a core curriculum for children who are at Piaget's concrete operational stage of development, that is, for the Primary child or those who are in the first years of a Middle school. But if account is to be taken of the changes which characterise the transition from child to adult it becomes evident that the activities associated with the young fade, the teenager, no longer tied to concrete operations becomes more interested in and able to handle abstractions, he becomes more socially conscious too, develops deep interests in specific subjects and shows a growing concern for real life issues.

This is not to deny of course that for some the interest in physical activity in one form or another will persist and opportunities should obviously be provided to allow those individuals to pursue the activity of their choosing and achieve the highest level of expertise possible. The numbers of children retaining an interest in gymnastics and who therefor opt to continue to participate regularly may well increase since the comparatively recent upsurge of interest in Olympic gymnastics, due in part to television coverage and the charisma of some champions, has had significant repercussions in schools. Children of all ages are joining the increasing number of gymnastic clubs springing up in most major cities. In the hands of competent coaches able children are becoming extemely skilful at a relatively early age, skilful that is in the range of movements which constitutes Olympic gymnastics. Such competence can be likened to that of children who attend private classes in ballet, speech or who receive individual music tuition.

Teachers, however, who have a good grasp and understanding of material and are able to apply their knowledge imaginatively should be able to ensure that such expertise is extended to include a versatile, adaptable, inventive and autonomous approach to gymnastic problems so that the individual's skill repertoire is fully extended.

The appeal of gymnastics for such children probably lies not only in the acquisition of increasingly complex skills but also in its newly acquired aesthetic orientation and maybe it is towards this consideration that its claim in education may shift. Few would deny that there is an element in a well composed and finely executed gymnastic sequence that is capable of sustaining aesthetic appreciation, and physical education teachers who perceive as part of their role the sensitising of individuals to aesthetic values both as performers and spectators may well view gymnastics as an admirable vehicle.

However, if gymnastics is to be regarded as part of aesthetic education then two crucial questions emerge; the first − is gymnastics the best, that is the most effective and most rewarding, vehicle through which to extend the aesthetic experience of the individual, and if this is answered in the affirmative then the second question must be posed − how must teaching be modified so as to bring this about? For to provide situations capable of prompting an aesthetic response is not sufficient. Teachers must in addition make a conscious effort to encourage, guide and develop perceptual discrimination, judgment and appreciation and in turn cultivate the critical skills and procedures required to express such distinctions. These problems, fraught with difficulty as they are, are ones which nevertheless must be considered seriously if the case for gymnastics as an aesthetic mode of experience is to be argued convincingly.

But for the majority of Secondary school pupils alternatives to the gymnastic lesson may need to be provided, for example, lessons which as suggested above include opportunities for conceptualisation and reflection. Activities such as Yoga, T'ai Chi Chuan, Judo, Aikido, Karate all have a gymnastic "flavour" but are more stylised and as well as promoting flexibility, mobility, strength and cardio-vascular fitness also require of the performer precision, poise, sensitivity, fluency, grace, control, concentration and may in addition provide the individual with a clear sense of purpose, significance and meaning. Many teenagers would no doubt readily accept, even welcome, the formalised discipline demanded from participants in such activities and while some could become interested in their historical backgound and/or philosophical basis others might prefer to study the physiological effects of, for example, Yoga or T'ai Chi.

For schools offering C.S.E., "O" or "A" Level courses in Human Movement Studies such suggestions could provide an excellent basis for study involving of necessity both practice and related theory. They might also contribute to a Health Studies course which included, for example, such topics as the relationship between exercise and relaxation, exercise and fitness, exercise and obesity, considerations of weight and figure control or specific and personal conditioning programmes. Such courses, while incorporating practical activities of a gymnastic nature, could take account of the maturation of boys and girls in the Secondary school and involve a re-orientation of purpose from the seven to twelve years old physical education programme; exclusively geared towards acquisition and refinement of skilled performance, to a more sophisticated study of the relationship between physical activity and modern living.

SUMMARY

The aims in teaching gymnastics suggested in this book clearly indicate the gradual shift of focus from *the contribution gymnastics can make to the achievement of psychomotor competence* in the early years through the stage where *refinement and exploitation of skill is linked with understanding of the relationship between the structure and function of the body* during the Middle years of schooling, to a point when the individual is capable of *appreciating not only the complex nature of skilled movement in general but also within the context of gymnastics* in its widest sense.

Statements of curricular aims of necessity imply particular views as to the purpose of education and as such will inevitably provide a constant source of controversy and debate.

Teachers will continue to make their own decisions regarding the selection of material and method and neither pressures from the Government, curriculum theorists, parents nor pupils themselves, necessarily oblige educators to take steps to meet demands for change.

There will also be those who relinquish all responsibility and capitulate completely to the demands of older pupils, satisfied merely to "keep them occupied" or "keep them entertained". There are others who will rely on their teaching experience, status in the school, ability and general charisma and persist, in spite of all opposition, in teaching the traditional programme of activities throughout the school. Many in fact will unquestioningly offer pupils such activities regardless of current trends in curriculum theory and no doubt restraints such as costly specialist equipment and facilities, local and national traditions along with staff expertise or interest will continue to dominate thinking and restrict the action of a great number of physical education teachers. But there are some physical educators who, along with their colleagues teaching, for example, mathematics and science, will be prepared to modify, adapt and re-orientate their knowledge in order to improve their practice in the light of current information regarding educational and pedagogical issues. Such teachers, also aware of pupils' changing interests, attitudes and values, will be prepared to look and to see how these might relate to their own convictions regarding education.

For the benefit of all teachers who are conscious of the need to reappraise present practice and who are genuinely searching for a rational basis to their decision making the authors have sought to be critically constructive; on the one hand indicating particular weaknesses in certain justificatory arguments for the continuance of gymnastics in schools while on the other offering alternative courses of action. There is no doubt that much time, thought and energy will need to be expended in such a search but surely this is to be regarded as a professional responsibility, more particularly at a time when teachers are required to look beyond the confines of the classroom and the school to the wider context of the community and society. Nevertheless it is to be assumed that able teachers who are convinced about the value of the subject they are teaching and

committed to a particular course of action will be as successful in teaching new courses as they were in teaching previous
ones.

CHAPTER 3

Lesson Planning and Organisation

When planning a lesson in addition to the movement material, the space, equipment and the time available have all to be considered as well as the age and aptitude of the class. The space varies from playground or hall to a fully equipped gymnasium and while some schools are well supplied with a variety of small and large apparatus both fixed and portable, others are limited to small apparatus. The time allocated could be from twenty minutes in some schools to forty-five minutes or longer in others. It is realised that this time is often shortened when Juniors, for example, have to be assembled and led to the playground or when apparatus has to be collected from other classrooms. Similarly in the Middle and Secondary school, children may arrive in small groups having travelled from other parts of the building. Time has often to be allowed also for complete changing and showering and the teacher, with all these considerations in mind, will plan his lesson accordingly.

It is advisable to outline a series of lessons around a particular theme or themes selected with the specific needs of the class in mind and it should be noted that while one main theme is being developed, related subsidiary themes will naturally be referred to. Each lesson in turn can then be planned in more detail, building on the teacher's observation and the results of previous work.

Whatever the length of lesson, the proportion of time allocated to floor and apparatus work has to be considered. This, however, must be left to the discretion of the teacher in relation to the theme, its stage of development and the needs and abilities of the class. Throughout the text the teacher's attention is drawn to considerations such as the need to introduce apparatus early in the exploratory stages of themes, for example, twisting and turning, since the opportunities to exploit this idea are thereby greatly extended. Indeed the teacher may find that certain aspects of themes are better introduced using apparatus, as in inverted balance, and that it is only when individuals have acquired a degree of confidence that work on the floor can profitably be attempted.

The proportion of time therefore allocated to work on apparatus must be decided by the teacher but in addition to the considerations mentioned above the fun and excitement which are such obvious outcomes of work on apparatus should not be ignored.

LESSON PLANNING

Since the style of teaching suggested in this book has a problem-solving basis, setting tasks and the wording used are of vital importance. During any lesson the teacher's initial objectives as well as his observations will do much to determine the progress of the class in terms of tasks set or problems posed.

Tasks and wording.
Tasks can be divided into those which invite children to *explore* a number of possibilities and those which are more *explicit* and focus attention on particular aspects of the theme being taught. Within this simple framework tasks can be:

orientated towards a *body* part emphasis,
predominantly concerned with whole body *action*,
directed towards the *track* or pathway to be followed, or
concerned more with the *quality* of the movement.
A teacher therefore has at his disposal a number of possible choices on which he may base the tasks he sets. For example, a task can be either exploratory and body orientated or explicit and body orientated, it can be exploratory and track/action directed or explicit and track/action directed and so on.

It has already been pointed out that the wording of tasks is most important and these should be such that initially

```
    E X P L O R A T O R Y
E  ┌──────────────────────
X  │
P  │   Body
L  │   Action
I  │
C  │   Track
I  │   Quality
T  │
```

they promote immediate and individual response and therefore they need to be concisely worded. The teacher's intentions however will determine whether tasks either are to be *exploratory* and therefore more open-ended or more *explicit* and therefore more specifically worded. The interplay between the use of these two types of task is central to the "problem-solving" style of teaching referred to earlier and teachers should recognise the relevance of each for particular teaching situations.

FLOOR WORK is discussed under the headings of *preparation*, *movement training* and *conclusion*.

APPARATUS includes considerations of *provision* and *tasks*.

Floor Work

PREPARATION

This has a dual purpose. The need to prepare the body for the vigorous, energetic movements which follow later in the lesson is obvious, whereas the mental preparation is often neglected.

In the Junior or Middle school, where children are frequently active and where other lessons involve moving about the classroom, the need to prepare physically is not so necessary. In the Secondary school, however, where children spend most of their day behind desks and are less inclined to physical activity, it is essential that the body is brought to a state of readiness.

At any age the need for mental preparation should not be overlooked. Movements in everyday life are on the whole automatic since actions once learned are rarely consciously considered and in other lessons although movement may be involved in the activity, whether this be drama, pottery, rural science or home economics, the focus is not on moving. Once inside the hall or gymnasium, however, the child is expected to think in movement terms since the problems and challenges set involve selection and decision making of a practical nature. This brief period at the beginning of the lesson is therefore a useful transition.

In gymnastics the trunk as well as the limbs are used in travelling actions, necessitating the preparation of all body parts to receive weight. Continuity of action should be stressed where movements follow fluently, each influencing the next. This may be done with a gradual increase of speed and energy until, towards the end of the preparation, a climax is reached. In the course of the lesson since the spine will be arched, curled, stretched and twisted, these movements should be experienced both on the floor and in flight during the first few minutes. Particular care should be taken to ensure that the trunk is activated and this will result if movements are related to the centre of the body. The preparation of feet and ankles should be stressed, as these are the main ejectors and receivers of weight.

Actions at first may be on the spot, but these should quickly develop into travelling. Once locomotion takes place an awareness of the general space is needed; control in speed and changes of direction will be required in order to avoid others also moving within the same area. Judgment and ability to adapt to changing situations becomes important and should be stressed in these first few minutes.

Preparatory tasks

As only three or four minutes may be devoted to this preparation, a task can often be set, the answer to which fulfils a number of the requirements mentioned above.

Task 1.—Invent a sequence of bodily actions, *e.g.* run, jump and roll.

Task 2.—Explore a series of repetitive actions, *e.g.* rocking, rolling or transferring weight from hands to feet.

Task 3.—Experiment with ways of travelling using various

methods of weight transference, *e.g.* rolling, sliding, flight or step-like actions.

Task 4.—Work close to the ground, travel over the floor and use it to gain height. This task could be related to a familiar theme, in this case variation in level.

Task 5.—Work on a variety of actions which start and end on the feet. This task could be the exploratory process of the main theme of the lesson, *e.g.* transference of weight.

Task 6.—Practice a sequence begun in a previous lesson. This depends on its suitability; a sequence involving resiliency would require a brief preliminary preparation, whereas a transference of weight sequence could be started immediately.

Task 7.—Repeat or recall a sequence or action phrase particularly enjoyed.

The first few minutes of the lesson, therefore, are particularly valuable, for when the brief periods allocated to gymnastics in some schools are considered, the stress must surely be in making maximum use of the time. Wherever possible the aim should be to get the children into the habit of moving quickly to the lesson, of changing and beginning purposeful work straight away.

MOVEMENT TRAINING

The aims of gymnastics, that is of improving and extending skilful control and promoting understanding and appreciation within this process are all applied in this section to work on the floor. Subsequently such knowledge and skill can be employed to advantage when working in other situations such as with a partner or on apparatus.

This part of the lesson begins when a new theme is introduced or the theme embarked upon in previous lessons is recalled and developed. During the exploratory stages of a theme children should be given time to experiment within the tasks set and it is during this period that the teacher must be particularly alert and observe the needs of the class as well as those of individuals.

Examples of helping the whole class

The specific teaching points the teacher chooses to make

will of course be closely related to:

the lesson theme;

the age and previous experience of the class and

the immediate needs of the majority.

He can help both to extend the skill level and improve the quality of the work by, for example, drawing attention to one or more of the following:

the variations possible within any given task;

the body parts which are important in achieving a particular skill;

simple biomechanical principles involved;

the degree of tension or appropriate time changes required to execute a skill or transition most effectively;

the body line.

He can also highlight the particular quality of what is being attempted, for example, a flight or balance experience, not only by the use of voice but also by his choice of words.

Examples of helping individuals

This may be done in several ways and only a few are listed below.

A child may need:

assistance in order to clarify a particular movement or sequence of movements;

reassurance, encouragement or physical support if he lacks confidence;

to be presented with progressively demanding challenges if he is underachieving or lacks the ability to challenge himself further,

while the majority will certainly respond positively if praised for genuine effort or improved performance.

The teacher should be completely familiar with his movement material and realise that the less able and less inventive his class, the more he may be required to take the lead in the exploratory period, introducing a few new ideas at a time. With a more experienced class it may only be individuals who need specific help.

Apparatus Work

With the two aspects of floor work completed, the next part

of the lesson can now begin: work with or on apparatus, small and large, or work with partners or groups. The time allowed for apparatus work should include that taken to erect and clear it away. Therefore organisation should be such that the minimum amount of time is taken on grouping and the handling and placement of apparatus.

Throughout the rest of this chapter specific reference is made to Junior, Middle and Secondary schools, as variations in type of equipment used, space available and organisational considerations of each age group are so great. However, teachers who are teaching gymnastics to beginners will find that, irrespective of the age of the class, much of the elementary material in relation to apparatus will be applicable to their work, while teachers in Primary or Middle schools may discover that relatively young children are very capable of attempting work classified as advanced. In the remaining Chapters therefore reference is made only to "young" or "older" children or "experienced" and "inexperienced".

PROVISION OF APPARATUS

Primary and Middle school

Prior to suggesting a number of specific needs of Primary, Middle and Secondary classes in terms of the provision of apparatus there are certain general points outlined below which might be helpful for the teacher to keep in mind whenever he is planning apparatus, regardless of the age group of his class.

Apparatus, as distinct from floor work, makes particular *demands* on the performer. It requires greater skill, for example, to work on *narrow, raised* and/or *inclined* surfaces and as such requires greater courage and confidence in the mover's own ability. When apparatus is introduced problems are posed in relation to judgment of *distance, height* and *timing,* while mobile apparatus makes greater demands on *balance* and requires added *control* and *co-ordination.*

On the other hand work using apparatus has certain *advantages* over moving at floor level.

It may provide:

a *gripping* area and therefore afford added security;

a *raised* surface and therefore assist flight experience;

a clear *objective* and therefore provide a sense of achievement;

added *interest* and *excitement* and therefore act as a powerful motivating force;

a range of *surfaces*, flat, angled, rounded, narrow and high and therefore offer greater variety of action.

Apparatus is also capable of being adapted to suit a variety of abilities and presenting progressively difficult challenges so that experienced individuals can choose the situation which both answers the problem set by the teacher and is best suited to their capabilities. Wherever possible young children should be given opportunity for swinging, climbing, balancing, clearing heights, negotiating small spaces, jumping on and off apparatus, sliding and twisting. Children of this age love to clear obstacles or to run and jump from a height, therefore at least one piece of apparatus should make provision for this type of activity. Where large apparatus is scarce, use can be made of the stage, stage blocks, steps and low tables which are strong and stable, while inclined forms or planks attached to stools are also suitable for this activity.

Climbing and swinging are favourite activities of this age group, and this should be remembered when providing apparatus for an energetic Junior class. In those schools possessing climbing frames, which may include ropes and trapeze, children should be encouraged and helped to use these imaginatively and with increasing skill. It is at this age that, because of their build and strength relative to their weight, boys and girls alike can explore the great range of gymnastic activities possible using these situations. As well as being provided with large spaces to work in, children should also be expected to work in a limited area, learning to control their bodies within that space. Raised hoops or skittles and canes can be used to provide different spaces to get over, under and through. Work with a partner and a hoop can be sufficiently challenging, even for older children, if the teacher and class appreciate the variety of ways a hoop can be held and the number of ways in which it can be used (*see* Chapter 11 on Partner Work).

It should be remembered that nine, ten and eleven year olds are frequently talented gymnastically and where it is possible and appropriate the level of work demanded from these able children on apparatus should be concomitant with their abilities.

Middle and Secondary school

When children are capable of working competently on a number of different pieces of apparatus height and distance can be varied considerably and more can be expected in terms of moving fluently over increasingly complex arrangements. Sequential work restricted to single pieces of apparatus presents the able performer with new problems and places different demands on his inventiveness, ingenuity and skill, while mobile apparatus can be introduced as yet a further challenge.

Finally individuals or small groups may select their own apparatus and decide on its placement in order to meet the task set by the teacher and variations of this idea can be found on p.211 in Chapter 12.

TASKS ON APPARATUS

Primary and Middle school

When setting tasks using individual pieces of apparatus with Juniors who have little or no movement experience, the class needs the security provided by directed work. Children whose movement vocabulary is limited cannot be expected to take advantage of a wide choice. The teacher must give confidence by guiding them carefully and skilfully through the exploratory stages of any theme. One method of helping children over this initial period is to give *action* tasks. With a class experimenting with ways of travelling, the following *explicit* tasks could be given:

Apparatus—individual mats.

Task 1.—Run and jump over your mat lengthways.

Task 2.—Run and jump across your mat.

Task 3.—Take off from two feet or one foot as you jump.

Task 4.—Jump up to your mat and roll across it.

Task 5.—Hop from side to side.

Task 6.—Run to the mat, jump over it and turn in the air.

The teacher can then give *exploratory* tasks which encourage the class to find other ways of approaching the mat and to discover alternative methods of crossing it. The teacher may then note that not many children are attempting to take weight on the hands, therefore further *explicit* tasks might be set:

> *Task* 7.—Using your hands on the mat, make your feet go from side to side.
>
> *Task* 8.—Roll towards the mat, cross with the body stretched, jump away and turn. Repeat, but this time cross the mat taking weight on a different part of the body.

Both show a transition from an *action* task to one which is more *body* orientated.

Having allowed the children a great amount of freedom, the teacher may then set progressive challenges based on the results produced. One might include both movement and action tasks.

Once children have built up a considerable movement vocabulary on small apparatus, the progression to work with two or three pieces arranged in a circuit will be simple.

When introducing large apparatus for the first time the children need not necessarily be given a task. Time is needed to get the "feel" of it and find ways round, so it might not be until the following lesson that any problems are set.

At first it is usual for the whole class to work on the same task related to the movement idea experienced in previous work on the floor. Once other themes have been introduced, groups can be expected to work at a variety of tasks. It may be possible for the whole class to be working on the same theme, *e.g.* time changes, but stressing different aspects on apparatus—*see* Chapter 9.

Placing and arrangement of apparatus and the setting of subsequent tasks is not a haphazard affair. It requires considerable care, thought and understanding of what each piece and arrangement provides, always relating this to extend the movement experience of the class. Often one sees the same arrangement of apparatus used for a complete term, with different tasks set. This is possible, but all too frequently results in disappointing work with little variety or originality.

Children at this age have an abundance of energy and apparatus and tasks should always relate to their needs and characteristics.

Middle and Secondary school

As with young beginners, when the work is new it is helpful to give the whole class the same task. For example if the aim is to help the class to discover various ways of using hands and feet to travel the following *exploratory* tasks could be set:

Apparatus—one form, two mats.

> *Task* 1.—Experiment with the variety of ways in which the hands may be placed on the form (*e.g* gripping the sides, placed on the form symmetrically, one on the form and the other on the floor, using hands alternately, placing the hands far apart or one in front of the other).
>
> *Task* 2.—Explore the various take-offs and landings (this will include the five basic jumps).
>
> *Task* 3.—Combine the use of hands and feet, (*e.g.* hands placed near each other on the form, feet kept astride the form, or using alternate hands to bear weight, keeping the feet together and making them go from side to side).

Once new apparatus is introduced time should be given to enable the group to work freely exploring heights, surfaces, approaches and landing points.

Having established a number of groups all working on different arrangements of apparatus a variety of tasks needs to be set. Gradually as new movement ideas are introduced these tasks may vary, with half the class working on the new theme while the remainder have tasks related to work covered in the past. A class having worked on speeds and varying direction and level, for example, may begin to consider flight. Out of six pieces of apparatus, three could be related to the new experience while the other groups work on time changes, level and direction. When partner work is begun after perhaps half a term, then the apparatus could change and tasks also. Three groups could proceed to work on various aspects of partner work, while the teacher may decide to retain two sets of apparatus concerned with flight and the one remaining group may have a choice of task, stressing time changes, level or direction.

With groups of experienced third or fourth years the whole class could work on one particular theme, but explore different aspects, *e.g.* the class has worked on speed changes in an elementary way and used time variations on apparatus, groups could now b'egin to experiment with the more advanced aspects, climaxes, accents, repetitive rhythms, time changes within a single action. Therefore six simple pieces of apparatus could be provided to cater for the various aspects of the one idea—*see* Chapter 9.

ORGANISATION

In this section *groupings* for apparatus, *handling* of apparatus and ways of *arranging* apparatus are discussed.

Primary and Middle school

When children come into the Primary school they have rarely worked in set groups. Infant groupings are constantly changing and children wander freely from one piece of apparatus to another whereas in the Junior school the child will eventually be expected to work with others on a set piece of apparatus, to help erect and clear away, handling it carefully and safely. He will have to learn to share apparatus to take his turn, to help others and to remain with the same group for perhaps as long as half a term. All this needs careful and consistent training and should be introduced gradually. When a class is ready to work in small groups the teacher could use the following progression as a means of arriving at work in fours and it is realised that this may take as long as a term if the class has only one period a week.

Lessons 1-2.—All work with individual mats.

Lessons 3-4.—All work with individual hoops.

Lessons 5-6.—Half the class work with mats and half with hoops, changing over within the lesson.

Lessons 7-10.—Half the class collect a mat and the other half a hoop, each child finds a partner and both work with the mat and hoop, arranged in a way the teacher feels appropriate.

Lessons 11-14.—The two may work with a mat and hoop plus another piece of small apparatus, *e.g.* a rope, two skittles and a cane, a chair or a stool.

From this point onwards a combination of two groups will produce groups of four with two hoops, two mats, stool and skittles available, which if carefully placed could provide a challenging situation for six- or seven-year-olds.

When children begin to work in groups the numbers should be kept small and the provision of apparatus such that each individual may work continuously with only a brief rest between turns. Two means of ensuring that activity is continuous and time wasting queues avoided are:

(a) to provide a return activity so that children are helped to use the floor space around the apparatus to advantage and in an inventive way, and

(b) to point out that individuals need not adopt the same starting point and that a variety of approach and pathway can be selected.

A group of four children could therefore work simultaneously using apparatus skilfully and with the added task of avoiding each other. This may mean that the teacher has to make the children aware of places where overtaking or passing is possible and encourage a pattern of working away from and back towards the apparatus rather than maintaining constant contact with it. This in turn necessitates the provision of adequate space surrounding each arrangement and allowing maximum freedom of approach.

Once children have had the experience of working in fours or fives, different groupings can be attempted, e.g. if apparatus is used which involves height, children of similar size may be required to work together, whereas if partner work is being introduced the teacher may decide to allow friends to work with each other.

In the lower Junior school, boys and girls mix freely in classroom activities as well as in the hall or playground and, where this continues throughout the school, they work together easily on apparatus. In this situation, each contributes towards an appreciation of the others' qualities of movement, the girls "catching" some of the speed and dash of the boys' movements, the boys assimilating the finish and precision of the girls'. This may not be the case in all schools and teachers may feel that at a certain age Primary and Middle school boys have preferences not held by girls of the same age and arrange groups and apparatus accordingly.

Middle and Secondary school

If young children have experienced sharing apparatus and

working with others the process of grouping at a later stage does not provide such a problem. Thought should be given, however, to the composition of groups, which may vary according to the theme of the lesson. Friends may work together in the early stages, but once bars, for example, are introduced it may be necessary to re-arrange groups according to height.

If partner work is being explored it may be profitable for friends or those of comparable ability to work together although this is not necessarily so, and the added demands involved in working with a variety of partners is dealt with in more detail in Chapter 11.

Although the teacher should realise the limitations and disadvantages of groups remaining constant over too long a period, the stability which springs from working with the same people should not be ignored and should certainly be taken into account if group work as a theme is being tackled.

Handling of Apparatus

Primary and Middle school

When children are first introduced to work with apparatus, the teacher should insist that the equipment is handled with care. Children, on the whole, will respond and take a pride in doing a job well, and can be most precise when this is demanded. Apparatus trolleys and containers, well labelled, help to keep the apparatus tidy and general preservation of valuable equipment can be engendered.

Given sufficient training it should be possible for Juniors to erect any apparatus they are going to use, and this should be regarded as an integral part of the lesson. Lifting, lowering and adjusting apparatus with others gives practical experience of manipulating objects; it requires co-operation and can be used to stress the care of apparatus and a sense of responsibility.

Middle and Secondary school

Accepting the fact that children in the first year at either a Middle or Secondary school will have come from a variety of "feeder" schools where the movement experience and equipment used will have differed widely, it is best to assume that most of the fixed and portable apparatus will be new to the majority. It should therefore be the policy to introduce this gradually, with every child learning to handle each piece of apparatus safely and efficiently.

First years can be taught quickly how to carry mats and forms, with special reference made to mats that must not be folded and attention drawn to mat handles, which should be used. The two children carrying forms should realise that each has a responsibility for the other, and that they should be both alert and aware of other children who may move across their path. Care should be taken to draw attention to the placement of mats so that they neither overlap nor produce gaps when placed together. When mats are used for landing purposes the class should be made aware of the need to place them sensibly in relation to the task.

Relatively quickly the class can be shown how to get out hanging ropes, as this is the easiest piece of fixed apparatus to manipulate. Wheeled apparatus also could be handled and stabilised. This will include in most modern gymnasia a box, buck and horse; but when these pieces are not mobile then the children should be helped to carry them efficiently and this will include carrying layers of the box. One or two layers of the box are frequently needed and so the dismantling of this piece of apparatus must be covered even with certain wheeled types. Time spent in this early stage in training children to handle apparatus is certainly not wasted, in fact much time and anxiety will be saved later in the year, when the teacher feels secure in the knowledge that any apparatus can be handled efficiently and safely by any child in the class.

Apparatus such as bars, window ladders or hinged wall sections which involve uprights, wedges and pegs should be dealt with most carefully. The whole class should be shown how the apparatus works and should be taught the correct order of movements. The appropriate number of children can then be selected to get this apparatus out and put it away for the next few weeks. Each new piece which is introduced should only be erected in order that the group can use it; there seems little point in getting out apparatus only to put it away again.

By the end of the first year every child in the class should be able to handle any piece of apparatus. The class should also be made aware of apparatus that needs checking during the period of work, *e.g.* they should realise that pegs and wedges may work loose, that mats may become displaced and that hooks on inclined forms need to be checked from time to time. The teacher, however, should undertake the ultimate responsibility for the safe erection and placing of apparatus.

Arrangement of Apparatus

Primary and Middle school

Organisation of apparatus before the lesson can sometimes reduce the amount of time taken in setting it up. In lessons where small apparatus is used it can be placed around the hall or playground, avoiding confusion when children collect equipment, and allowing the pace of the lesson to be maintained. Where several pieces of small equipment are to be used by each group, they can be placed near the area of erection. This could be done by a few children before the lesson begins, or the teacher himself could distribute the apparatus during the first few minutes of the lesson.

The introduction of several pieces of apparatus can be organised in different ways. The simplest of these is to keep the apparatus the same for all groups.

Apparatus—individual mat, a rope and two hoops.

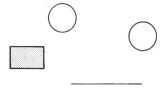

One progression from this is to use the same apparatus but to re-arrange it slightly for each group.

Apparatus—as before.

Another progression is for half the class to work with the same apparatus while the other half works with different apparatus, *e.g.* with a class of forty, divided into ten groups of four, five groups could work with apparatus *(a)*, and the other five with apparatus *(b)*.

Apparatus *(a)*—individual mat, a rope and a hoop.

Apparatus *(b)*—individual mat, two ropes, skittle.

The next stage is reached quickly when the larger pieces of apparatus are introduced. This can be done reasonably simply in three lessons, the teacher helping two groups in each lesson to add their large piece of apparatus to whatever small apparatus they may be using, *e.g.* one group may be working with the mat and hoop and two ropes placed on the floor.

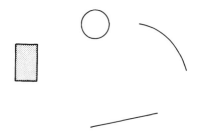

The teacher may feel that this group needs a piece of apparatus to jump over and adds two stage blocks; the re-arrangement might lead to the following.

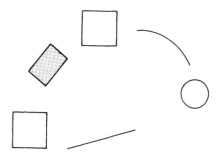

This simple re-arrangement will not take long and the teacher could easily deal with the introduction of two new sets of apparatus in one lesson. Therefore, after three lessons, six new arrangements will be completed.

When more complicated apparatus is arranged, speed of erection has to be considered. All the apparatus may have to be collected from the same store room, in which case the children setting up apparatus farthest away from the store cupboard should be allowed to collect their apparatus first, arrange it and begin work, as soon as the teacher has checked for safety. Whenever possible each group should erect and put away the same apparatus for several weeks; having worked on other pieces they return to put the original away. Thus each group becomes proficient in handling one piece of apparatus before learning to deal with something new. This could be referred to as their "home" apparatus and will save valuable time, as, with constant repetition, efficient organisation of handling and placing will result.

With children who have worked in groups for some time on large apparatus, re-arrangements of this can present certain problems. One way of overcoming difficulties in organisation could be to use the "card" system. The group is handed a card on which is clearly marked:

(a) the apparatus to be collected,
(b) the placement,
(c) the task.

A master card can be made available and placed in the classroom, hall or gymnasium so that each group can see its position in relation to the general working space and other group arrangements.

A leader can take responsibility for following the instructions, although the group as a whole help arrange the apparatus. The teacher can later check spacing and more exact placement. When groups are ready to change over, either the card can be left behind or the leader can remain to explain the task.

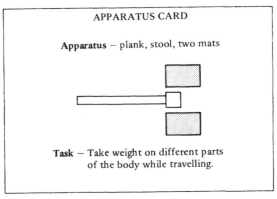

APPARATUS CARD

Apparatus — plank, stool, two mats

Task — Take weight on different parts of the body while travelling.

If space is limited in the hall or playground, it is advisable to provide some groups with normal working space and to limit others, thus allowing at least half the class, in turn, to work with the necessary freedom of unhampered movement.

Middle and Secondary school

Various arrangements of mats and forms will suffice as apparatus for the first few weeks. These can be used most

effectively and provide challenging situations.   With six
children in a group, arrangements could be:

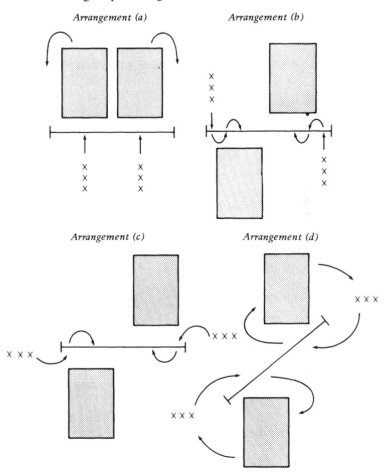

Arrangement (a)   *Arrangement (b)*

Arrangement (c)   *Arrangement (d)*

As new pieces of apparatus are introduced, *e.g.* bar, horse,
ropes, these can be used by three groups of children while the
remainder work on a new arrangement of forms and mats. A
changeover could then take place during the lesson so that
each child has a period of time on apparatus which is familiar
as well as on a new piece.

Once the class has learnt to manipulate ropes, box, horse
and buck, these pieces can be combined with forms and mats

to provide a more challenging situation, and if arranged care-fully can help the children explore the many and varied approaches towards, and pathways over, the apparatus. Where the top layers of the box only are being used, in some types the lower ones can also be utilised with forms inclined either broadways or lengthways on.

Forms will usually suggest ways of approach and mats provide landing areas, therefore if apparatus is placed in a straight line the results will be limited, whereas in the following arrangements a variety of starting points and tracks present themselves.

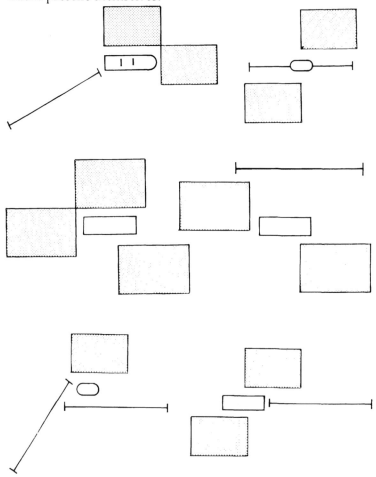

As with Junior classes, groups should set up and put away their "home" piece of apparatus for several lessons, becoming familiar with this and saving valuable time.

Each group should be given at least one change of apparatus each lesson and care should be taken to see that the selection of consecutive pieces varies. This will ensure that heaving is not followed by swinging, nor will work which includes a box immediately precede a similar arrangement with the horse. The usual method of change-over is to rotate thus:

but it may be necessary where, for example, three bays of hinged wall apparatus are being used, to change across the room:

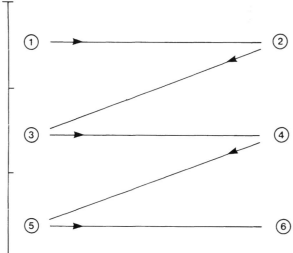

CONCLUDING ACTIVITY

Just as the children need to be prepared bodily and mentally at the beginning of a lesson, so at the conclusion it is equally important to bring them together in order that they may recover from the excitement and stimulation of work on apparatus.

Slow, controlled movements may be suggested by the teacher, perhaps linked with symmetry or stretching and curling. If tasks are given which involve lowering parts of the body or balancing and returning to the normal standing position, points concerning poise and posture can be mentioned. Generally movements should be selected where the body moves as a whole, maintaining equilibrium and continuous contact with the floor.

This brief unwinding period at the end of a lesson enables the teacher to draw the class together, so that the session ends with the children as a unit rather than dispersing in small groups. It also means that as soon as one group has finished replacing apparatus, time need not be wasted waiting for others. The class can be trained to begin the concluding activities in any space available, individuals eventually selecting their own movements.

CHAPTER 4

Movement Observation

Movement is transient and in the teaching situation is rarely recorded by notation, by still or cine-photography or by video-taping, although the latter does offer exciting possibilities as a teaching and learning aid when it is available. However, one way in which teachers and children can widen their knowledge of movement is by trying to see and to understand what is happening while it is happening. This is movement observation, the degree or depth of which will vary with the circumstances. Observation could be defined as seeing with understanding since in observing there is an active seeing of movement involving sympathetic participation by the observer rather than watching passively, or merely looking.

OBSERVATION BY THE TEACHER

It is vital for a teacher to observe children, whatever the subject or situation. It is through observation that the successful teacher assesses the moods, attributes, needs and potential of individuals and groups. The observation of children moving should not be confined to the gymnastics lesson. Observing children at play, as they move around the school, in the classroom, as well as during other physical education activities, can be most valuable. In such situations the experienced observer can learn much about the children he is teaching through an understanding of their movement behaviour.

The Junior or Middle school teacher has a unique opportunity to know his pupils since he is with them in most of their activities. In the selecting of gymnastic material this knowledge could help him to widen their movement experience and cater for their movement needs. Similarly, what the Junior or Middle school teacher observes in the gymnastic lesson should be of value in the classroom, contributing to a better understanding of each child.

The physical education specialist whether in a Middle or Secondary school has the opportunity to become an expert observer of movement. However, he must realise that he is seeing children in one situation only, revealing though that situation undoubtedly is.

In the teaching of gymnastics it is particularly important that the teacher should observe well. Within a lesson the movement experience is guided by a series of tasks, each dependent upon the reaction to the preceding challenge. This demands acute observation. The difficulty arises sometimes when there are many answers to a given challenge and often the teacher will have as many different solutions offered as there are children in the class. Moreover, there are few set responses and usually the work is exploratory. Unless the teacher is able to observe adequately it is unlikely that either he or his class will gain satisfaction from working in this manner, because of his inability to select, use and develop what he sees.

The ways in which a teacher observes his class *generally* are obvious, for example, young children coming from a crowded classroom to the relative freedom of the hall or playground may immediately show a desire to exploit the space. Seeing this the teacher might give action tasks, such as running and jumping, before expecting more controlled work as in balancing. Prior to the gymnastic lesson an older class may have had a period where concentrated mental effort has been demanded. When the children are beginning to warm up their actions may appear lethargic and through a quick assessment of their mood the teacher may decide to devote time to a guided enlivening of the body.

At the same time the teacher is also concerned with more *specific* and immediate problems to which observation can provide the answer. When a task is set it is vital to see from the response if the movement ideas involved have been understood and are being used profitably. As a result of his observation the teacher may need to clarify the task for the whole class, or it may be that individuals require further help. (*See* p.25 Chapter 3).

Sometimes the teacher may be looking for those whose response to a challenge is worth showing to the rest of the class. The way in which children can be helped to observe is dealt with later, but here the connection between observation by the teacher, selecting and "showing" is seen. In his selection the teacher is often setting a standard of work, therefore he should choose children whose work contains something of value. Demonstration in its narrowest sense (that this is the only way to answer the problem) is not normally relevant to this way of teaching gymnastics. However, it is often expedient to select children to show their work to the rest of the class. It may be that several children are chosen because

(*a*) they have variety, or

(*b*) they have a particular point in common.

For example, perhaps two or three will choose to balance on hands, but each arranges the rest of his body differently and the teacher may wish to point out such possibilities to the rest of the class.

Selection by the teacher necessitates quick observation and this must be trained consistently. The poor observer may find himself faced with exciting activity from which he is unable to extract anything of significance. A pitfall to be avoided is that of looking only at those individuals who can be expected to find a worthwhile solution. If the same children show their work lesson after lesson, while the less spectacular or less able individuals are precluded, then the opportunity of the latter making a valuable contribution is lost. The skilled observer should be able to watch and select from the whole class.

Although of necessity much of the observation is concerned with the class or groups, opportunities should be taken to observe individuals. Through observation over a period of time the teacher can build up a valuable "movement picture" of each child. He can learn to recognise and help not only the skilled and the able but also the apparently lazy, the foolhardy, the accident-prone, the nervous and those lacking confidence.

To the beginner it may appear as if this method of

teaching is only for the expert observer of movement, but this is not so. All teachers are continuously adapting and adjusting their teaching material to the needs and reactions of their classes and observation is one way of gaining feedback. However, it is stressed that to be successful in this work it is essential to observe movement consciously and to set out to train this faculty deliberately.

Framework for Observing Gymnastics

In the teaching of gymnastics the understanding of movement and movement observation are complementary; each will gain from the other.

When beginning to observe the teacher may see only those aspects of movement to which he himself is sympathetic and stresses in his own work. However, just as the successful teacher avoids imposing his own movement preferences on his class, so the sympathetic observer must train himself to look for all aspects of gymnastics and not be confined by his own movement experiences.

The following is suggested as a framework upon which the teacher can build his observation of class and individual. Although it is hoped that teachers will endeavour to observe children moving in many situations, it is recognised that most observation of necessity takes place during a lesson. The headings are basic, being valid for both general and specific observation. The examples given are from typical gymnastic situations that a teacher might observe.

In the observation of gymnastics the teacher's attention is upon four separate but related aspects within the context of the theme being taught.

1. *Body.*—The observer determines *what* the body is doing by looking at part, parts and the whole.
2. *Space.*—The observer sees *where* the body is moving by noting levels, directions and pathways.
3. *Speed, Tension and Energy.*—The observer considers *how* the body is moving by assessing the speed, tension and the energy expended.   •
4. *Relationships* (with or without contact).—The observer notes the relation between the body and the floor, apparatus, partner and group.

1. BODY

In gymnastics many different actions can be distinguished. Some of these involve the body as a whole, while in others a part or parts are more important than the rest. It is the interplay and relation of parts to each other and to the whole body that concerns the observer.

Curling, stretching, twisting and jumping are examples of actions normally involving the whole body. Through observation the teacher determines if this is so or if parts are omitted from the action. In curling, for example, the head and parts of the spine are often neglected. When stretching, children find difficulty in feeling this action through to their extremities and so what is happening to the hands, head and feet needs to be observed. In flight children often anticipate the landing through lack of confidence and this results in the upper half of the body inhibiting the flight, for instead of carrying on the upward thrust of the legs, the stress is downward, the focus being towards the landing area. The teacher who observes these "bodily happenings" can then help his class to be more aware of what the body is doing and this should lead to more sensitive work.

In many actions, although the whole body is alive to the movement taking place, some parts because of their function have more emphasis than others as when sliding on the trunk occurs. The part of the body in contact with the ground is held in position, while one or more of the limbs provides propulsion by vigorous pushing or pulling. In such situations the limbs carry the main stress of the action. When a balance is held and then the weight transferred, the part that is to bear the weight assumes importance as it is prepared and placed in position.

In observing what the body is doing the teacher can see the extent to which the class needs further help. Similarly the next step in teaching can be determined. If the task "experiment with balancing the body on asymmetric or uneven bases" is given then in this challenge what the body is doing is being stressed and the teacher would find his teaching points by observation based on the following questions.

(a) Are all the ways of producing an uneven base being

used—*i.e.* two unlike parts from different sides, or two parts from the same side, or two like parts placed unevenly?

(*b*) Are individuals challenging themselves to the full, trying difficult inverted balances?

(*c*) Are the balances being held or moved through?

(*d*) Is there an awareness of what the rest of the body is doing above the base?

Whenever the challenges are specific to the body or action tasks are given, the teacher should always observe the body first, for this ensures that the teaching point is pursued and developed. Often there is a temptation to deviate. An inexperienced teacher might follow the initial task with the suggestions that the class "add variations of speed". This shows not only lack of movement understanding but also poor observation. Progressions are based on the response to each challenge and it is unlikely that a class concerned with experimental balances will indicate a need to consider speed changes as well.

When observing the body, in addition to looking for the interplay between the parts and the whole, as in climbing a rope, the teacher must take other considerations into account. Sometimes the lower half is more important than the upper, as in taking off from the ground. Often one side is stressed more than the other, as in the beginning of a cartwheel. The movement possibilities of the body are virtually limitless and persistent observation is required to recognise what is happening and then to act upon what is seen.

2. SPACE

The need to observe the body in space during floorwork depends upon the task set. The spatial aspect may be of primary or secondary importance.

In an introductory task of "alternately travel high in the air and low along the ground" the first observation would be directed towards the use of level. It would be necessary to see if the high and low levels were being exploited or if the movement was taking place in a meagre extension of the medium level. In another introductory task of "travel on different body parts" it would be essential to ensure that this was happening before observing the use of directions. Levels, directions, pathways and body shape are often incidental to the main action of the body during floor work. Just as observation should not be directed immediately towards these aspects, so the class should not consider them until clarity and understanding of what the body is doing are shown.

When a spatial theme is taught there is much to observe. In the task of "travel, using different directions" the observant teacher may see many variations. Some children will remain on an habitual pathway, such as circling the hall or gymnasium, and while on this track will travel forwards. backwards or sideways. Others will concentrate on a varying track composed of lines, zig-zags, loops and curves which changes their front in relation to the space, but retain one direction, usually forwards. Having realised this the teacher might re-word his challenge or decide to bring the different responses to the attention of the children by selecting several for them to observe.

Apparatus is often arranged so that each individual can select his own actions and pathways and here the teacher can observe if these are well correlated. One child might always approach each piece along a straight pathway, another only change direction on the floor between apparatus and in both cases limited use of path and track would probably narrow the choice of action. A third child might adjust and shift about on apparatus in order to change direction because of an inappropriate arrival. If a teacher can observe such situations and understand the resulting difficulties he should be in a better position to offer constructive help.

3. SPEED, TENSION AND ENERGY

Although what the body is doing is often of prime importance, how the body acts is also a vital consideration. When the speed of an action is assessed it is not sufficient to decide if the rate is quick or slow, although this is a beginning. Phases where acceleration or deceleration occur, as well as the rhythm and climax in a sequence, must be noted. A child may not get on to a high box because he has failed to build up his speed during his approach. Another child may be unable to hold a balance on a bar because he has not appreciated the need to decelerate into the balance. Actions such as jumping for a rope, helping a partner to achieve flight, landing on a narrow surface from a swing on a rope, are often inefficient because the timing is poor. A teacher who can appreciate when lack of timing defeats the aim of an action will have taken the first step towards being able to give positive help to his class.

Many children fail to get over high apparatus with weight on hands. This is because they cannot produce a strong energetic action in the upper part of the body or they do not realise that any change in tension is required. A teacher who by observation can pinpoint the reasons for inefficient and unsuccessful actions is more likely to help the performers than one whose comments remain at the "try harder", "get over next time" level.

Sometimes the speed, tension and energy may appear secondary to what the body is doing. When attempting to roll for the first time, young children can be helped if attention is drawn to the action of the body rather than the tension and energy required. On acquiring the skill, however, it may be of great importance to stress these, particularly when the roll is one of a series or part of a sequence.

In many actions there is an equal stress on what the body is doing and how it performs the action. The take-off to achieve flight from the ground is a typical example. The action of the body is from flexion into extension but unless this is done quickly and with considerable energy no flight results. Similarly, the flight phase itself can be impaired by too little or too much tension. In observing ineffective take-offs and flight the teacher must see which of these vital ingredients is missing or over-stressed and help accordingly.

4. RELATIONSHIPS

In gymnastics the body can never be considered wholly in isolation. Whatever the action there is always a relation between the body and the ground or apparatus or other people. This relation, whether it results in contact or not, is often taken for granted. A class showing little sensitivity in this respect usually reflects a teacher who has failed to observe well and consequently has done nothing to remedy the deficiency.

In getting on to a small box from the floor with weight on hands a young child may not appreciate the importance of where he places his hands. He may put them too near the edge, so that there is little room for the rest of his body, or too far away, so that he is unable to take weight on them. Having observed this the teacher could suggest that he climbs on to the box and finds out where to place hands and feet in relation to each other and to his intended action.

An older child trying to swing from a rope to land on a box top some distance away will often continue to push the box from him not realising what is the cause. The teacher who has observed that the approach is from the side instead of from above the box, or that the body is rigid instead of "waving up" over the feet on contact, is likely to help the child to be successful.

Another child attempting to roll along the top of a box might do this as if on a mat and consequently roll off the end. The teacher who observes that this child is unaware of the relation between the length of his back, the size of his roll and the space available may well be able to give constructive help.

In many activities which involve flight on, off and over apparatus, the placing of the hands determines what the rest of the body can do. When helping an individual in this situation, the teacher should observe where the hands are placed on the apparatus and how the rest of the body is used in relation to the hands, as this often indicates the reason for an unsuccessful attempt.

It is mentioned in the chapters devoted to partner and group work that such situations should not be explored until the teacher considers the class capable of benefiting from them. The decisions to start such work will be based on knowledge of the class which has been built up by constant observation. Once working with others is taking place the teacher needs to be particularly alert to see that this is progressing in a safe and profitable way. Concern for the partner or group has to be encouraged and fostered by the teacher.

When observing a small group trying out ways of lifting and lowering each other the teacher needs to be alert to the amount of give and take that is necessary. He will see those who readily adapt to being one of a group and those who find this difficult. From his knowledge of the individuals concerned the teacher should know the best way to deal with the situations observed.

When a selected challenge is presented to his class the teacher will normally know which aspect to observe first, whether "what" the body is doing is more important than "how" it is acting, and what to look for subsequently. However, it is often necessary to consider the movement as a whole to determine its main characteristics. This happens when a teacher finds that a child has decided what he wants to do in answer to a movement challenge but for some reason is unable to carry out his intention. If the teacher is to help within the context of the situation he must observe what the child is trying to do and how he is setting about it, or, if this is not clear, ask for a verbal explanation.

The teacher must decide from his observation and knowledge of movement what are the essential characteristics of the action or series of actions, the inherent factors that make it what it is. For example, in jumping the body is always thrust into the air and although the jumps may vary in size the thrust is always present to a greater or lesser degree. Once these are determined they must be seen in relation to the child and how his attempt differs from that which will bring success. When these movement discrepancies have been discovered the teacher is in a position to give positive help.

In addition there are certain biomechanical factors which determine to a large extent what the body can and cannot do in, for example, flight and balance. If a teacher's observation is supplemented by such knowledge, which becomes of increasing relevance as advanced work is reached, then his teaching should be enhanced.

It is through an understanding of movement, a knowledge of each child and observation that a teacher should be able to relate the movement essentials of actions with the ability and movement characteristics of the individual.

OBSERVATION BY THE CLASS

Just as observation is vital to the teacher so children can be trained to observe and helped to profit from what they see. The visual is important as a way of learning and can help to widen an individual's movement vocabulary. Points which would otherwise remain obscure might be clarified by watching classmates tackling a common problem. It is in seeing the variety of ways in which a challenge can be met that the scope of a movement theme is appreciated. This is particularly so when observation is followed immediately by the children exploring ideas for themselves.

Beginners usually try to copy the actions seen but later children can select from the movement ideas observed and make them their own by modification and adjustment. The movement imagination is usually stimulated and enlivened by observation.

Through observation children begin to appreciate their own movement characteristics in relation to those of others. The child who naturally moves quickly can, by observation, recognise slow, unhurried movement and with the teacher's help this can be developed into an awareness of moving slowly when work is resumed. The ability to perceive one's own movement preferences as well as limitations can be vital in the establishing of a self-concept.

When beginning observation with a class the teacher has the possibilities of:

(a) selecting two or three individuals whose work is worth showing to the rest of the class,
(b) dividing the class in half so that each group in turn observes and moves, or
(c) dividing the class into couples so that each child observes his partner in turn.

In (a) the observation is focussed but the children showing may be self-conscious. In (b) the observation is more dispersed but those moving are unlikely to be inhibited and each child experiences both situations. In each method the teacher has two groups both of which need guidance in order to benefit from the experience.

The observers should be given one point to look for first, e.g.:

"What parts of the body take weight?"

"Is there an increase or decrease in speed?"

"Which direction is being stressed?"

As skill in observing increases more than one movement aspect can be considered, *e.g.*:

"What is the essential difference between these two sequences?"

"What have these people in common?"

"What varying relationships occur in this group sequence?"

After observation the children should be able to make a brief analysis of what they have seen and offer constructive criticism.

The performers may need to be told beforehand that their work is to be seen. This ensures that they are prepared both mentally and physically. Some children obviously enjoy being selected and this often provides motivation for further effort. Others lack confidence but the teacher can do much to create an atmosphere of mutual help so that this difficulty is eventually overcome. Having shown his work the mover should receive helpful comments. Occasionally sequences may be selected that only partially fulfil a challenge and this situation must be handled carefully by the teacher. It can be successful only when the relationships are such that the performers have confidence in the sympathy and understanding of the teacher and the rest of the class. Then an exchange of ideas and views can be valuable and do much to add to an understanding of the movement problems involved.

The third method, *(c)*, has advantages in that the observation is directed towards one person and the performer is unlikely to be self-conscious. It is essential in this situation that the teacher gives specific observation points. The disadvantages are that some of the work seen may not be particularly good and the teacher cannot easily check that all the couples have profited by the experience.

After observation it is usual for the class to work again at the same task. The children who observed must be given a chance to put what they have seen and learnt into practice. Those who performed will have been given help which they can now implement. When the whole class resumes work it is an excellent opportunity for the teacher to see if the time spent on observation has been worthwhile.

The teacher should be able to use class observation appropriately. In starting a new gymnastic theme observation is of little value when the work is at the early exploratory stage. Too much observation too soon can be limiting. In partner and group work observation usually occurs during the working out of ideas and this not only enables movements to be matched where applicable but also fosters sympathetic work.

Observation is one way in which appreciation of logical movement can be gained. Younger children are invariably able to see this first in the work of others before they can make a similar assessment of their own efforts while older children are able to appreciate the varied work of others of differing abilities.

Through observation children are given the opportunity not only of watching others but also of adding to their own movement understanding. Furthermore, when children observe perfected gymnastic work it is a situation in which the teacher can guide and aid their critical faculties by pointing out those features and attributes of the performance that might be termed aesthetic.

The place of observation in any one lesson needs careful consideration. Abused it can kill the pace of a lesson, used skilfully it enhances both movement and understanding. Young children and beginners do not need to observe often but older children can profit by short intensive sessions. The experienced teacher will probably include observation by the class of floor or apparatus work or both in most lessons. It is through an understanding of the value of this way of working and seeing it in relation to teaching gymnastics generally that a teacher is most likely to use observation profitably.

CHAPTER 5

Elementary Body Management

The ability to control and manage the body would appear as one of the main essentials in any given movement situation. In gymnastics this is certainly a prior consideration. Children must first be guided towards an awareness of the capabilities of the body. Later they can be helped to acquire greater mastery, in terms of control and management, which in turn leads to heightened enjoyment and satisfaction that springs from increased skill.

Unlike learning a foreign language, gymnastic movement is not new to the beginner; children, however young, will have already gained a degree of bodily skill, and will certainly have experienced joy and satisfaction in moving. Once the child is placed in the learning situation, however, although use is made of movements he has already mastered, the emphasis now is on a growing consciousness of what the body is doing, of how it is moving, and where it is going. Once this awareness has been fostered, the children's habitual movements are extended to include new skills, which when mastered, become part of a wider, more varied movement vocabulary.

The term "body awareness" has over the years become for many something of a meaningless catchphrase; in this text, however, it denotes the individual's experiential identification of himself in terms of his body concept within the gymnastic environment. In everyday life it is essential that each individual evolves a basic vocabulary of habit actions such as walking, sitting, eating and dressing. Although the kinesthetic sense has been involved in the acquisition of these skills, conscious effort in performing them lessens until eventually they become habitual and a conscious awareness of what is happening is no longer required. In civilised communities, interest in and awareness of movement are on the whole subdued; movements tend to be restricted and restrained, children's actions become inhibited and retarded through contact with a variety of adverse situations. It is this awareness of what the body is doing, how one part moving affects the whole, and the relation and interplay of body parts in action, which must be stimulated if the movement vocabulary and ability of individuals is to become enriched and vital.

The following elementary themes of Locomotion, Stillness, Weight Bearing and Transference of Weight all involve guiding children towards an awareness of the body in action. Although there is variety within this selection certain correlations exist but for clarification each aspect is considered in isolation. It should be noted that these are dealt with in a form of progression so that each new idea utilises the knowledge and skill acquired in previous work.

LOCOMOTION

Material

Locomotion, that is travelling, is achieved by the transference of weight from one part of the body either to the same part, or to another in succession. This is normally brought about by weight being transferred on to one or both feet, as in stepping, running, hopping or skipping, but in gymnastics this is by no means the only method. Ground can be covered by hands supporting the weight of the body while feet overtake or follow, as in cartwheels and crouch jumps. Another way of travelling is where contact with the floor is maintained and the body kept curled and compact as in rolling. This can be experienced on a variety of body surfaces and in any direction. When the body is ejected into the air and flight takes place the body travels through space, and although this too is usually achieved from feet to feet, other parts can be used to eject and receive body weight. The body can also be moved from one place to another in a sliding action, which usually involves large surfaces such as front, back or hips. In this instance, although travelling results, the body itself may or may not move, for after the initial impetus the shape can change or the position be maintained whilst sliding takes place.

This aspect of gymnastics is a relatively simple idea and, when the basic methods of travelling over the floor have been explored and understood, cannot profitably be sustained for any length of time without recourse to more demanding situations. Extensions can be made to the original notion through the use of apparatus which greatly increases the range of practical possibilities or the focus of attention can be re-directed towards the more cognitively demanding themes of weight bearing and transference of weight.

Teaching

Although locomotion is a fundamental aspect of gymnastics, in the early stages of introducing this work to children, it is dealt with in a very elementary way. It is, however, a useful starting point, as most young children are interested in ways of getting from one place to another, and are concerned with the "going" and with the parts of the body used when covering ground.

It is sufficient at this stage to experiment in order to discover the various possibilities of travelling, and experience should be given in the number of ways in which feet or hands and feet are used in conjunction. Children should be encouraged to use the trunk as well as parts of the limbs on which to progress and resulting actions should include such activities as crawling, sliding, running, hopping, leaping, rolling and rocking. (*See* Plate 1.)

Young children are often unable to change readily from one action to another and therefore transitions are rarely achieved fluently. Nevertheless most children between the ages of six and nine enjoy repeating the same action several times and can be encouraged to do this. In some cases a rhythm will be established in repetition which children find most exciting and satisfying. Action phrases including various ways of travelling can be introduced at this stage where simple transitions only are involved and weight bearing is restricted to a limited number of body parts. These can be related to the movement preferences of children of approximately this age, for example, most will choose to run, jump, land and slide to a stop; or run, jump and turn in the air, land and roll; whilst to run, dive and slide would be a characteristic action sequence for many.

PLATE 1

A later development for older children is to combine travelling actions, where they learn to move easily and with agility throughout a sequence, with a number of body parts taking weight in turn.

Teaching points concerned with receiving and transferring weight are dealt with later in this Chapter.

Apparatus

The elementary aspect of locomotion will mainly concern Primary teachers; however the specialist teaching in the Middle school or first year Secondary pupils may be tackling the same theme, but will probably have a greater variety of apparatus with which to work. Suggestions for work on apparatus are, therefore, dealt with separately for Primary classes, although the principles of providing apparatus for work on locomotion remain the same for any age group.

Opportunities should be given for travelling with specific body parts suggested—

1. on the feet,
2. using hands and feet,
3. on hands only.

or the stress can be on bodily actions—

4. by sliding,

5. by rolling,
6. by gripping and releasing alternately.

1. LOCOMOTION ON THE FEET

Obstacles should be provided to jump over, to get in and out of, or on and off, along, or to go from side to side.

Primary.—Apparatus such as canes or hoops supported on skittles, individual mats, ropes and jumping stands, planks, chairs, low tables and steps all provide suitable challenges for this activity.

Middle and Secondary. —Forms used both narrow and broadside upper-most and slightly inclined, mats and mattresses, will initially give sufficient opportunity for experimentation with the basic idea of travelling using feet only.

2. LOCOMOTION USING HANDS AND FEET

Classes can be introduced to the idea that hands can lead while feet follow, that hands can lead and feet overtake, that hands and feet can be on the same or on different levels, and that limbs can work together or alternately.

Primary.—Ladders or planks used horizontally or inclined on stools or climbing frames, ropes or nets where the children can clamber, scramble and climb, would be sufficient to stimulate a variety of ways of travelling using hands and feet. (*See* Plate 2.)

Middle and Secondary.—Forms used as suggested in 1. above, bars or any type of hinged wallbars, ropes or wooden climbing ladders, planks or box tops should present beginners with a sufficient variety of experimental situations.

3. LOCOMOTION ON HANDS ONLY

As it is impossible for the majority of children to travel on the floor taking weight on hands alone, this possibility can be more thoroughly explored on apparatus. There are two essential differences between using the hands on the floor and on apparatus. One is that on apparatus the hands are able to grip, an action impossible on a flat surface. Secondly, whereas on the floor the body must be above the hands if

PLATE 2

these are to support the weight, on apparatus it may be suspended below the weight bearing part, an entirely different experience. Also if inversion is involved, as it will be in most cases, the stability and support provided by apparatus is invaluable for those lacking confidence and may even furnish the initial experience of what it is like to maintain inversion while moving onto, off or over the hands. On the apparatus the hands may move alternately, but not overtaking each other, as in swinging sideways along a bar, or one may pass the other as when the body travels in the forward and backward direction. Hanging, swinging and climbing are all activities which will answer this task.

Primary.—Rope or other types of ladder, balance bars and climbing frames provide the children with opportunities for exploring the above ideas.

Middle and Secondary.—Both boys and girls can experiment on bars at hanging height, travelling along and moving in all three directions, while some may also be able to travel up a rope or across a number of ropes taking weight on hands only. Boys, for physiological reasons, will probably be able to enjoy the challenge of swarming a rope or ladder using hands alone and will also produce a greater variety of methods of progressing along bars.

4. LOCOMOTION BY SLIDING

This activity can occur on raised surfaces, parallel or inclined to the ground. The body can be pulled along the top or underneath with a number of bases being used.

Primary.—Balance bars or planks inclined on to stools or raised between two stools, slippery topped tables or forms offer situations for pulling up, sliding along or down a variety of surfaces.

Middle and Secondary.—This is not an activity that needs to be pursued at any length but it can be dealt with adequately using inclined forms at a variety of heights and bars at hip level to give first years an experience of what is involved in the action.

5. LOCOMOTION BY ROLLING

If this action is to be attempted with confidence on apparatus, then it must be preceded by sufficient practice at floor level. The apparatus at first should be comparatively low, broad and stable and the individual can be expected to complete the roll on the apparatus provided, *i.e.* arrive on the apparatus, roll and then get off. The obvious progressions are dealt with in the section on transference of weight and in Chapter 12.

Primary.—Table tops, wide planks, forms and stage blocks, are surfaces that can be used, provided they are not too high and are safe in all respects.

Middle and Secondary.—Children should be given the opportunity of experimenting with a variety of rolls on surfaces such as forms and box tops, and the majority should be able quite quickly to progress to some of the more difficult ways of rolling on apparatus, a point developed further on pages 79-83.

6. LOCOMOTION BY GRIPPING AND RELEASING ALTERNATELY

This has already been mentioned with reference to travelling using hands only. In addition to this, however, children can be helped to explore other parts of the body capable of gripping, which can often be used in conjunction with hands to produce locomotion. These parts such as the toes, instep, back of the knees and front of the hips cannot be included as weight bearing bases when travelling at floor level, but once on apparatus can, if necessary, support the whole weight of the body.

Primary.—Any type of climbing frame, ropes or supported ladders and poles are suitable for children to experience the gripping action which is such a basic requirement for all work on apparatus. (*See* Plate 2.)

Middle and Secondary.—Climbing frames, hinged wall bars, window ladders, bars, ropes, bar boxes and the horse pommels offer a variety of gripping situations.

In the early stages of planning apparatus for young children, the teacher's responsibility is to set the scene, providing an environment which will lead the children towards experiencing the greatest variety of activities possible. Provision should be made so that many of the above activities can be included, with each piece of apparatus dealing with a particular aspect of locomotion. Once the class begins to work on apparatus the teacher can help to widen the children's movement vocabulary by setting simple tasks that stimulate them to discover new ways of using the body when travelling. He must also ensure that each child is encouraged to work on several different pieces of apparatus and eventually tackles them all over a period of time.

With older classes, apparatus can provide opportunities which include various methods of travelling, *e.g.* gripping and sliding, sliding and rolling, jumping over and rolling, while they can also be encouraged to travel over the apparatus using many pathways, travelling in a straight line, making a circular or zig-zag track.

Plate 3 shows a class of seven-year-olds working on locomotion with a variety of apparatus.

STILLNESS

Material

The body travelling and the body in stillness must both be experienced if full awareness and skilful management are to be gained. Although in the early stages of mastering stillness it will suffice that movement is checked and body weight

PLATE 3

controlled, it should be realised that stillness does not merely mean "to stop moving". It implies that movement is held so that the muscular tension involved in arresting an action and maintaining a still position can be experienced. This should be considered as an "active pause" or a "dynamic stillness" rather than cessation of movement; a positive attitude should be adopted towards stillness in which appropriate tension is felt and used to maintain the position of the body.

Actions can be brought under control and stopped in several ways. If the body is kept compact and all angular parts contained within the curved shape, once the body is set in motion movement will be continuous until a time when the original momentum is lost. If, however, a flat part of the body is released, such as a forearm, and comes in contact with the floor, or the body itself is uncurled, movement will be interrupted. At that point, an abrupt stop can be achieved providing sufficient bodily tension can be produced to check the forward momentum at the moment when weight is received on the flat part.

An abrupt stop is not always necessary, however, and stillness can be brought about by a gradual loss of momentum. When a landing from a jump which involves tilting or turning takes place, there may be a momentary loss of control and inability to halt the action unless the distribution of body weight is adjusted appropriately. One way of recovering equilibrium would be to continue to move, following the direction of body weight, and to round the body so that weight can quickly be transferred from feet to other parts. This may result in a rolling action where the speed can be controlled when the feet come into contact with the ground and grip the surface, or it may lead into a rocking motion where momentum can slowly decrease, resulting in eventual stillness.

Speed can be checked and a running action brought to a stop by ejecting the body into the air. In order to achieve the upward thrust at take-off the forward lean of the body has to be altered. This opposing of the forward momentum by the vertical ejection is instrumental in initially checking the speed of the run. When considering the most effective way of stopping the action, it will be found that of the five basic jumps, the two to two is the most efficient. In a double take-off an initial interruption of speed occurs while one foot meets the other and the body is brought into symmetry. On landing on two feet the body is more likely to be controlled and stable and an immediate stop can be effected in two ways. Firstly, movement can be checked through space when, on landing, the body flexes and regains the normal position with the landing and recovery taking place on the same spot. Secondly, there can be a complete cessation of movement when a gripping action on arrival holds the landing position. The first method of stopping is the more usual and the resulting resilience should be encouraged. The second is occasionally resorted to in some emergency landings, for example, where space is limited and also used in the more advanced aspects of flight into balance. In addition it is also a characteristic of landings from Olympic gymnastic vaults.

However, the more usual method of take-off and landing is from one foot to two. In this instance the asymmetrical running action remains unaltered in the take-off and it will not be until the feet come together in the air that symmetry is achieved, but ultimately this does take place and preparation can then be made for a two foot landing and, as previously stated, stillness may then result.

The stability and control achieved from a two foot landing obviously assists ultimate stillness. This may not be an immediate necessity and the performer may find it requires a following jump or number of resilient jumps in order to control fully the momentum gathered in the preparation and the actual leap itself. In this case speed can be lost gradually, the height and tension involved in the bounces following the landing will decrease steadily until full control is experienced and a stop is made possible.

Movement can be performed with either free or bound flow. Free flow is apparent in movements which are difficult to stop at any given point bound flow is evidenced when the control is such that actions can easily be checked. It will be recognised that in gymnastics free flow exists in certain ballistic situations but the attitide towards flow is mainly concerned with actions which are sufficiently controlled to allow for quick adjustment, adaptation or immediate stillness. In dealing with stillness it should be realised that the body control involved in achieving this is of great importance when considering safety in any movement situation.

Teaching

With young children, mastering stillness will be a major step in managing body weight. They have little inclination to stop actions, being mainly concerned with travelling; in some instances it is only due to the fact that they become exhausted that movement eventually ceases. In the early stages the teacher must be prepared to dictate the moment of stopping and yet not expect a common class response. Very few will be able to bring about anything but a gradual cessation of movement. Another way of helping children to experience stopping is to set situations where a natural stop occurs, as in sliding, swivelling and spinning. This could be developed by helping them to contrast the feeling associated with the gradual petering out of movement in these actions, with a deliberate stopping of a slide or a spin, and the resulting held position. The use of action phrases could prove effective at this stage, and words such as stop, grip, check, balance, interrupt and arrive, contrasted with pause, hover, rest, finish, decelerate, peter out and die away, used to produce variation in the quality of *becoming* still. Later, individuals can evolve their own phrases of movement and although this is a difficult stage, the teacher must be patient and persist, helping them to clarify the starting and final positions as well as paths followed and actions performed.

Once the initial stage of controlling the body has been mastered so that stillness results, children should be able to employ this ability in more difficult situations. They should become adept at avoiding obstacles and other children by stopping abruptly and be able to react to any situation requiring immediate stillness.

It is at this stage that weight bearing on different parts may be introduced. If this is attempted before children have been given sufficient time to become accustomed to the tension which has to be produced before stillness is achieved, the results will be disappointing and little satisfaction will be experienced. Stillness here will involve a deliberate interruption of the action and attention will be focused on the part or parts of the body bearing weight, rather than on the movements leading into and out of the arrival. There will probably be little or no feeling of the true balance or poise which will be developed when greater bodily skill has been mastered. The advanced technique involved in balance includes awareness of the manner in which the balance is achieved and lost.

Apparatus

The teacher of younger children is concerned more with action than stillness on apparatus, but the ability to stop or change direction to avoid others or obstacles is something that children must eventually learn to include in managing the body.

They can be helped to master the skill of checking movement by first experiencing the control required when changing direction. This can be accomplished with each child working individually on small apparatus.

Apparatus—individual mats.

Task.—Run and jump over the mat, turn and roll back.

Apparatus—a skipping rope on the floor.

Task.—Jump from side to side using feet only, at the end turn and come back using hands and feet to travel.

Apparatus—skittles and cane.

Task.—Run and jump over the cane, turn and slide back underneath.

Inclined planks can also help children to control the impetus of movement, *e.g.* when travelling up a steeply inclined surface using feet only or hands and feet, the speed naturally decelerates as the top is reached. As momentum is lost the action becomes more easily controlled and a pause is quite simply effected. Similarly, when sliding down, a stop at the bottom is the usual result.

Repetitive actions along forms, planks or benches can help the performer to appreciate phrasing and the child may choose for himself how many times the action is to be repeated before stopping.

Older classes can be expected to perform slightly more difficult tasks such as showing moments of stillness during a sequence on apparatus or experimenting with the task of finding different ways of arriving and holding a position on a given piece of apparatus. Wall bars, climbing frame, ropes, bars, box and horse can be used in the latter case.

Stillness should be seen as a contrast to locomotion and introduced in connection with travelling, but very soon the point at which the teacher can lead the class into weight bearing will become apparent.

WEIGHT BEARING

Material

Man's specialised way of using the body, that is, in the upright position, is not the main concern in gymnastics; the aim is to exploit the body to the full and to utilise its movement potential in a versatile manner. Weight bearing suggests that the weight of the body is above the supporting part; therefore on the floor weight bearing results in the body resting above a chosen base, although on apparatus, however, this is not necessarily the case. Locomotion and stillness are both related to this new idea because while travelling weight has to be controlled and held over the supporting part.

Many parts of the body are capable of taking weight but it will be discovered that some lend themselves more readily to producing a steady, stable base than others. The placement of these parts in relation to the floor and the rest of the body is also important. It appears natural in the early stages of weight bearing to use flat parts or parts that can be flattened such as shoulders, shins, hips, forearm and hands and to place these symmetrically.

As well as weight being equally distributed over two body parts which are the same, two or more different parts may be used which produce an equally steady base, *e.g.* a shin and hand, or a knee and two hands. The larger the base relative to the placement of the rest of the body, the steadier the position. It will be found when maintaining weight on two different parts that it is simpler to use right and left sides of the body. A progression will be to take weight on two different parts of the body using the same side, this requiring greater ability to control the body weight.

Later when greater skill has been acquired, the asymmetrical placing of parts can be exploited. Body weight can be held on a part of the trunk such as one hip or one shoulder, but a far more difficult challenge would be to produce an asymmetrical base using one or two limbs.

Rounded parts of the body can be used to support weight but when, for example, the head, knee or elbow forms part of the base other parts may be needed to stabilise the position.

While maintaining weight on one or more parts, the rest of the body may remain still or may move. In a cartwheel, for example, the body weight is supported on the hands, while the rest of the body, extended, wheels over the support. While bearing weight on the shoulders the body may be still or moving over the base while another part is prepared to receive the weight.

Weight may be received and maintained on parts of the body for a brief period or can be held for a relatively longer time, while the freed parts of the body are used, for example, readjusted to receive weight or to initiate the subsequent action. When taking weight either partially or wholly on the shoulders the legs may be symmetrical, reaching away from the ground, they may remain together or be far apart, one may bend and the other stretch, they may twist against the shoulders and circle, or one leg may reach out and the toe touch the floor whilst the other reaches up and away from the body. (*See* Plate 4.)

PLATE 4

Weight bearing must be considered in relation to body awareness: in the first instance, the actual contact with the floor of different body parts heightens the kinesthetic sense; secondly, when weight is taken on parts not normally used, the rest of the body is placed in a completely new situation and learning to manage the body in this novel position presents a considerable physical challenge. When inverted, for example, reach and mobility alter and a complete re-orientation is necessary.

Finally, in the consideration of work on apparatus which requires negotiating different levels and using the body's full potential, awareness and ability to manage the body in any situation is seen to be invaluable.

Teaching

The child, having explored methods of travelling and mastered the skill involved in checking an action, can now experiment with the idea that weight can be received on and supported by a number of different parts of the body. At first the teacher may need to help the class by suggesting that parts such as shoulders, hips and knees can bear the weight of the rest of the body. The children can then be encouraged to experiment for themselves, *e.g.* exploring the possibilities of weight bearing on all matching parts of the body, such as hands, forearms, shins. These activities will be performed first in isolation but once the children have mastered a few possibilities, they can then be expected to attempt to link travelling and stopping with reference to weight bearing. At this point the teacher may have to refer back to the ways of travelling previously experienced, if, for example, the children limit themselves to using hands and feet only.

In order to extend the experience of bearing weight on two identical parts of the body it could be suggested that hands, for example, can be placed near together, farther apart, side by side or one in front of the other.

A further progression might be to encourage the use of dissimilar parts of the body forming an asymmetrical base, and the class will probably produce many possibilities with this idea in mind.

PLATE 5

Older children could be presented with the task of discovering isolated parts of the body on which weight can safely be taken, e.g. one hip, one shin or one shoulder, or experimenting with the possibility of producing uneven bases which not only requires a more skilful adjustment of the body over the base but also results in a more precarious position being experienced anticipating problems which will be met later. (*See* Plate 5.)

Movement habits are easily established at this stage and it is here that the teacher can help children to experiment equally with right and left sides of the body so that weight is received as often on one as on the other. Throughout this aspect of the work the teacher should emphasise that antici-pation is needed so that parts which are to receive weight are prepared in the previous movement. Most children naturally prepare for action; this can be seen in the preparatory forward swing of the arms and backward movement of the top half of the body before attempting a handstand, and in the attitude adopted at the start of a race, or before a measured jump.

Once children have become aware of the possibilities of weight bearing and have experienced a fair proportion, they can begin to give some attention to the ways in which the rest of the body can be used while it is supported on any given base. Whilst weight is being borne on the hands, for example, the rest of the body can be elongated as in a hand-stand, it can be taken through a wide, stretched shape as in a cartwheel, it can be kept relatively compact as in a "Chinese" handstand, or crouch jump, or it can turn and twist in the air or move over the hands. These are only a few named skills and many others can be invented once the principle is grasped. (*See* Plates 6 and 7.) It is of interest to note that in Plate 6 the feet are high above the supporting hands whereas in Plate 7 in all but two cases this is not so.

During the exploratory stages of this idea, the child will merely be resting on the weight bearing part. Later the teacher should make the point that the rest of the body produces the appropriate amount of tension, enabling the performer to feel that the body is held in position over the point of contact with the floor. This is to ensure that the child maintains a liveliness within the body, alert to any action which might follow. Just as children's carriage is noted when in the normal positions of standing and sitting, so too, when weight is taken on other parts of the body, rather than allowing a collapse or slump, the teacher should encourage readiness. anticipation and a feeling of poise.

PLATE 6

PLATE 7

Up to this point the attention of the class will have been
directed towards the part or parts of the body providing the
base and the ability of the freed parts to be held or move in
a variety of ways.   When the child's attention becomes

concerned with ways of arriving, as well as resulting actions, this leads naturally into consideration of methods of weight transference.

Apparatus

When apparatus is introduced not only has a variety of surfaces and levels to be considered but also new parts of the body can now take weight, different combinations of body parts can be used as supports and as previously noted the body no longer needs to be above the supporting base.

SINGLE APPARATUS

When providing apparatus situations for this theme it is advisable to allow children time to work on single pieces of apparatus before confronting them with combinations. It is also helpful in the early stages to have the whole class using similar apparatus, *e.g.* everyone working on forms, or mats or a combination of bars and mats. Introducing this idea simply ensures that each child builds a considerable repertoire of ways of using single pieces of apparatus. This will be found of value later when groups are expected to work on a combination or circuit where forms, mats and bars are used in conjunction with larger apparatus.

Apparatus—mats.
> *Task* 1.—Cross taking weight on the hands, return with weight on another part.
> *Task* 2.—Approach with weight taken alternately on hands and feet, cross using parts of the trunk.

Apparatus—forms.
> *Task* 1.—Travel along the form with weight on hands, feet going from side to side.
> *Task* 2.—Using one part of the body on the form and another on the floor, travel from end to end.

Apparatus—bars (hanging height).
> *Task* 1.—Experiment with ways of getting from one end to the other using hands or feet or both.
> *Task* 2.—Experiment with hanging positions where weight bearing parts are the highest.

Apparatus—window ladders.

   Task 1.—Travel up or across using hands and feet alternately.

   Task 2.—Travel up or across using hands and a part of the body other than feet.

Apparatus—a low box.

   Task 1.—Move from one side to the other with one part only touching the apparatus, approach from any angle.

   Task 2.—Arrive on feet and get off with a part other than feet meeting the ground first.

COMBINATIONS OF APPARATUS

The following are examples of combinations of apparatus which offer varying levels.

Apparatus—two ropes and a mattress.

   Task 1.—Jump up onto one or both ropes; lower the feet gradually onto the floor. On contact with the floor transfer the weight on to other parts of the body such as knees, hips or shoulders.

   Task 2.—Preparation as in previous task but instead of lowering so that feet touch first, other parts of the body make first contact with the floor.

Apparatus—bar (medium height), low box, mat.

   Task.—Hands must be used to lead the body from one piece of apparatus to the other, therefore they must be the first part of the body to contact each new piece of apparatus.

Apparatus—bar (hip height), saddle, bar box, mat.

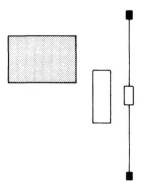

Task.—A different part of the body must make first contact with each piece of apparatus.

Apparatus—ropes, low box, two mats.

Task.—Swing from one or two ropes and land on the box on different parts of the body. Hands must be the first part to touch the mats.

WEIGHT TRANSFERENCE

Material

In weight bearing the focus is directed towards the part or parts which are to receive weight and to the rest of the body while weight is being maintained on a specific part. In transference of weight the stress is on what happens between weight being removed from one part and arriving on another; in other words, how the body moves between two points of support. Whereas weight bearing is concerned with relative stillness, transference of weight involves locomotion. Although there is a correlation between transference of weight and locomotion, the emphasis in teaching is different; in locomotion it is on the travelling, getting from place to place, while in transference of weight it is on the transitional movement between two weight bearing positions.

Transference of weight may be brought about by any of four ways:

1. rocking and rolling,
2. sliding,
3. step-like actions,
4. flight.

1. ROCKING AND ROLLING

This involves transference of weight on to adjacent body parts, *i.e.* along the spine as in forward and backward rolls, across the back as in sideways rolling, or on the front surface of the trunk. In some cases parts of the body which are not naturally adjacent can be made so. The feet can be brought near to the hips in a crouch position so that a movement where weight is transferred down the spine can be taken, without interruption, on to the heel and then the ball of the foot. The curved surface is thus maintained, allowing the rocking or rolling action already established to continue.

Rocking differs slightly from rolling in that in rocking the weight is transferred on to adjacent parts and is brought back again along the same line of supports in reverse. In rolling the weight is transferred along the spine and then eventually taken on to another body part. Rocking leads very easily into rolling and vice versa.

2. SLIDING

Sliding is another method whereby the body is transferred from one place to another while in constant contact with the supporting surface, but where it is not always true to say that weight has been transferred from one part to another. When children slide it is usually as a result of a run and dive, and in this instance the weight of the body is maintained on the same area, hips, side or front, while the body is carried along the ground.   The initial impetus comes from the speed generated in the run and dive on to the floor and locomotion will continue until this energy is spent.

When the body is sliding on a comparatively large area other parts may be used to provide added propulsion but it is only incidental that they bear part of the weight of the body.   In a sliding action on the hips the heels may be used intermittently to push and so maintain the original slide. While taking weight on the front surface of the body the hands, used alternately or together, can pull or push the body along the floor or apparatus and thereby assist the slide.

3. STEP-LIKE ACTIONS

Step-like transferences of weight resemble the process used in walking.   In considering the walking action it can be seen that from standing on two feet, weight is shifted on to one whilst the other is lifted, prepared and placed in a new position.   As weight is transferred on to the new support there is a moment when weight is equally distributed over the two feet, before being taken on to the foot last grounded and the process repeated, each foot overtaking the other in turn. Step-like transferences of weight can take place using a number of body parts, and in actions such as handstands and cartwheels this is the type of weight transference used, hands and feet alternately acting as supports for the rest of the body.

4. FLIGHT

In the three methods of transferring weight mentioned previously, contact with the floor has been maintained.   In the fourth method, momentary loss of contact with the ground is experienced and flight is achieved.

Transference of weight by means of flight is usually made from feet to feet or feet to hands, but flight can be gained by using other parts of the body.   In bouncing activities flight is achieved from, and weight received on to, the same body part.   Hands and feet can be used alternately with flight taking place between the push off from the feet and the landing on the hands or vice versa. This will be only momentary flight but the period in the air will be prolonged with the more skilful performer. Resilient landings, where the ability of the body to rebound is exploited, can be encouraged by bouncing and continuous leaping, while landing from a height and at speed may necessitate weight being transferred quickly on to another part. Use can be made here of the three other methods of weight transference.

Effective ejection, exploiting the flight phase and safety on landing are discussed in detail in Chapter 14 on Flight.

Teaching

Although transference of weight is a fundamental gymnastic theme, it will depend upon the age and movement preference of the class where the teacher begins. With a class of beginners who are lively and energetic the starting point could be with flight and sliding, whereas when older children are being introduced to this type of work, the teacher would be well advised to begin with step-like transferences. Wherever the start is made, all four ways should be introduced, each following reasonably quickly upon the other.

Flight and step-like actions involve the body in changing situations, whereas once the body assumes the curled shape and begins rolling, no such changes occur until the action alters. The bodily situation remains comparatively unchanged in sliding also, once the action is begun. In teaching transference of weight, therefore, it is as well to cover two methods in one lesson if a balance of activity is to be achieved, *e.g.* rolling and step-like actions could be taken together or activities which include flight and sliding could be combined.

1. ROCKING AND ROLLING

Rocking on parts of the body suited to this activity is a good preparation for rolling as the appropriate surfaces will be discovered and the necessity for rounding these areas will be appreciated. When rocking on the back it can be pointed out that slight rocking can be produced when only a small area of the back is used, or a more vigorous action is possible if the weight is transferred along the length of the spine. If the feet are tucked in and made to produce a continuation of line with the back and hips, the rock can extend to the heel and ball of the foot and the movement can then continue in reverse. Children can experience rocking not only on to two feet placed side by side, but also on to two feet with one placed in front of the other. This extends the rocking action slightly and is useful later in gaining continuity of action in recovery. If, for example, having completed a rocking action which is to be followed by a cartwheel or a handstand, the feet are placed one in front of the other, this will lead the body more smoothly into these actions than if weight were to be equally distributed over the two.

One activity which children might practise is rocking forwards and backwards on the back, gradually gaining momentum and including the feet in the action. When sufficient energy and speed have been gathered, the forward momentum can be directed either into a handstand or crouch jump or can be used to eject the body into the air. Having introduced the possibility that weight can be transferred on to feet at the completion of a rocking action, the child can now experiment with the idea that as the feet or the shoulders receive weight, the rest of the body is free to be redirected by a slight twist of the top or lower half against the fixed part.

Children should experience both curving and arching the spine and having discovered the possibilities of rocking on the back, the front surface of the body should be used. Some will find rocking along the front of the body, transferring the weight from the chest to the hips, quite difficult as this requires considerable strength and mobility. Once they have felt the two extremes of curling and arching the spine, some children will find this useful on apparatus. The active use of the upper and lower half of the body in this method of rocking should be encouraged and ways of leading into and twisting out of this action can be discovered.

A rocking action can also be effected by using the back from right to left of the spine, resulting in a side to side movement. The body, in this case, can be elongated or curled. The arms should be tucked in and the front of the body contracted so that the shoulders and back are rounded as much as possible, allowing maximum rocking to take place across the whole area. Once this has been mastered, ways of getting into and out of this position by transferring weight on to parts such as knees, forearms and hands can be explored.

Within rocking, the speed changes and the pauses which occur before a change of direction give the child valuable experience in that he can learn to increase and decrease momentum and discover the resulting rhythms, whilst the hesitation felt as the rocking action reaches the end of its path is perhaps a new experience for most. It is when performing such actions that children begin to appreciate inherent time stresses. It can also provide them with background knowledge which can be used to advantage at a later stage when changes of speed within actions are considered. With younger classes and to some extent with older children, this may not be so—it may not involve them in a conscious awareness—but if the teacher understands and gives the children bodily experience, this is sufficient until such time as they become capable of coping conceptually.

Although in pre-school play most children will probably have experienced rolling, they will not necessarily have explored all the possibilities. As a safety precaution the teacher needs to stress that in rolling the body as a whole must be curled, presenting a rounded surface to the floor. It should also be pointed out that all angular parts must be brought within the compact, curved shape of the body.

The head is an extension of the spine and as such must be included as part of the curve made by the rest of the body. Making this point to children attempting a foward roll will help most of them to achieve the skill smoothly and safely. Often when rolling children drop on to the back, which has been flattened as a result of the head instead of the shoulders first taking the weight. This can usually be overcome if the teacher leads the children to experience curving the spine and tucking the head while remaining in a crouch position on the feet. If, from this position, the hips are lifted and the feet push slightly, the head looking into the space between the legs, a roll will result. Others may find a roll over one shoulder easier and this can be achieved if, for example, from a position on all fours, the left hand is released and, with the head following, leads the body through the space made by the remaining hand and the knees. As the left shoulder comes level with the right knee, a state of unbalance occurs, and if weight is then taken on to this shoulder, an asymmetrical roll follows.

Some children will prefer rolling backwards over a shoulder, for once the hips are lifted off the ground and one or both knees directed over one shoulder, the balance of weight is such that the rest of the body easily follows and a roll is achieved. For those who do not feel sufficiently confident to attempt any of these ways, rolling sideways, with the body either in a ball shape or elongated, will be their first experience of continuous movement using this method of weight transference. Another method of helping children to roll is to suggest they use the experience previously gained in rocking. Rocking on the back, for example, can lead quite easily, for some, into either a forward or backward roll, where the body shape remains constant. For those who quickly master rolling itself, combining rocking and rolling and exploring all the possibilities of rocking into and out of a roll provides a different challenge.

If the teacher suggests that rolling can be performed in a number of different ways and allows the class complete freedom to practise rolls already mastered, or to discover new ways of rolling, each child is able to attempt the way or ways he finds easiest. It is then left to the teacher, knowing all the possibilities and ways of achieving them, to lead the class or individuals gradually towards an appreciation of what is involved in rolling. Young children gain satisfaction from repetitive action and during the exploratory period it could be suggested that consecutive rolls are attempted. Many will enjoy this activity, discovering that the rolls can take place within a limited area, *i.e.* a backward roll followed by a forward roll, or that travelling occurs when rolls are performed consecutively.

The more able the performer the greater the variety he should achieve, but each child, whatever stage he has reached, should be encouraged to perform asymmetrical rolls using right and left sides equally. Although most individuals have a preference for one side or the other, the ability to roll over either shoulder is of value later, particularly when performing a series of actions on apparatus or when working with a partner.

If sufficient mats are available when children begin work on rocking and rolling these should be used in the early stages, but as the action itself becomes more efficient and the children more confident, the necessity for mats diminishes and the tendency to limit the performer avoided. Care is always needed whenever children roll without mats and these should always be provided when using apparatus.

When children have become reasonably proficient their skill level can be raised by introducing a variety of specific tasks such as those which follow.

Task 1.—Lie face downward and, with the body elongated, slide into a forward roll. (This necessitates a strong levering action and as such is quite demanding.)

Task 2.—Lie on the back with legs together and stretched; maintaining this elongated position of the legs throughout, lift the legs and direct them backward towards the floor immediately behind the head; once contact is made resolve the roll by a sliding action which culminates in the body coming to rest face downward.

Task 3.—Explore the possible combinations of tucking, elongating, stretching, twisting and arching, for example — begin with legs astride, roll either forward or backward ending with the body tucked, or
— begin facing one direction; roll and prior to completing the roll effect a change of direction using a twist and perhaps arriving on a shin with the free leg extended.

Task 4.—Roll into and out of a handstand or headstand.

Task 5.—Rock on the front surface of the trunk into a one shoulder balance and roll out along or across the back.

Task 6.—Roll backward onto one shoulder and rock out along the front surface of the trunk.

Tasks 5 and 6 both necessitate a quick and agile change of body shape.

2. SLIDING

Although sliding is an activity which most children will have encountered it will usually have been associated with inclined surfaces. It can, however, be experienced on the floor provided that it is clean and splinter free. This is an important point whenever children are working but even more so when the action involves friction.

The class should first experiment with actions which naturally terminate in sliding, *e.g.* when starting from a position on the floor with weight on hips, a vigorous pushing action of the feet against the floor will set the slide in motion. A more effective push, resulting in a longer sliding action, becomes possible if the weight is taken on the feet, body curled, and only when the legs become extended is weight transferred to the hips. Junior children are remarkably skilful at launching themselves on to the floor and into a slide. This can be experienced from a standing position or, as happens more naturally, from a run.

While experimenting with actions which result in sliding, children incidentally discover that many areas of the trunk can be used. They can begin to combine the pulling and pushing action of the limbs with taking weight on different parts of the trunk, *e.g.* the weight can be taken on the front surface of the trunk and the hands used to pull and then push the body into a slide or, with weight on the hips, the hands and feet can push the body into action.

The more proficient children are, the greater the variety achieved. Most boys become expert at launching themselves on to the hips, front, side and thighs.

Some children naturally appreciate that the body travels better if it is streamlined and weight is taken on a comparatively small area. The teacher can help others to discover this by suggesting that they slide with whole surfaces of the body contacting the floor and then only part of this surface maintaining the body weight. In the latter instance the appropriate degree of bodily tension must be produced to hold the non-sliding parts off the ground.

3. STEP-LIKE ACTIONS

In step-like transferences many non-adjacent parts of the body can receive weight in turn. In rocking and rolling the child is concerned with large areas of the trunk along or across which weight is continually being transferred; now his attention is drawn to isolated parts of the whole body, and the combinations possible when using them in succession to produce locomotion.

It should be appreciated that in rocking and rolling movement will be continuous throughout the action. Step-like transferences may involve an interruption in the continuity of the action when weight is transferred on to flat or flattened parts of the body and maintained over that part for a brief period. This does not occur when the performer becomes more competent and able to repeat actions with ease and fluency.

The teacher should also realise that by the very nature of rocking and rolling activities, since adjacent parts are used in immediate succession, no variety of weight bearing parts is possible within one action. Step-like transferences, however, involve choice and therefore selection is necessary. It should be pointed out to the class that parts can be placed close to each other, as when transferring weight from feet to hands in a "Chinese" hand balance, or comparatively far away, as in a cartwheel. When the part which is being prepared to receive weight is to be placed to the side or a long way away from the supporting part, a considerable amount of bodily adjustment is involved, and great control is required before these skills are performed with any degree of fluency.

In some actions weight is taken from one part, received on another and placed back again on to the original part, as in handstands and cartwheels. Other actions can be accomplished which involve a constant change of parts receiving weight. In step-like transferences using hands and feet many variations are possible when combining the four limbs. The children should be allowed time to experiment, *e.g.* with transferring weight from two feet to two hands, two feet to one hand or from two hands to one foot. It is when dealing with step-like transferences of weight that the teacher should ensure that weight is taken frequently on the hands and in many differing situations. At an early stage children should be helped and encouraged to become increasingly confident in the inverted position. Tasks such as the following are challenges which will eventually lead most children towards becoming both competent and confident on the hands in inverted positions.

> *Task* 1.—Take weight on to hands and make the legs land in a new place. Land one foot after the other or two feet together.
>
> *Task* 2.—Take weight on the hands and get one foot high into the air. (In this case the same foot will be used to push and land.)
>
> *Task* 3.—Take weight on the hands and make one foot pass the other in the air. (This will involve one foot being used in the push-off and the other foot in landing.)
>
> *Task* 4.—Take weight on the hands and make the feet meet at some point in the air. (One foot will be used to push off and the landing will be made either on two or one after the other.)

This method of transferring weight requires a studied, deliberate action on the part of the performer, and means that the child must think in advance of the action he is performing.

4. FLIGHT

Jumping is an activity which the majority of children will have experienced previously as a means of travelling, but when flight is being introduced as one of the ways of transferring weight some of the considerations which are involved in flight must be dealt with.

With young Juniors it is sufficient that they play with the various ways already used earlier, such as hopping, skipping, bounding and leaping. Later the teacher can make the class aware that the feet can be used singly or together in both take-off and landing; that feet can catch each other up as in a single take-off with two feet landing, or that feet can pass as in leaping from one foot to the other. Together with bouncing along on two feet or one foot these activities will involve them, incidentally, in the five basic jumps. At

PLATE 8

this stage it is the going away from and meeting the floor again that is emphasised, not being in the air.

The next stage will be to introduce the idea that individual parts of the limbs can be stressed after take-off, *e.g.* knees can be accentuated when the legs become freed, one or both can be tucked up towards the chest and this can be done together or one after the other; feet can be lifted high into the air in front of the body one after the other, kicked into the space behind, or brought to the side. It will be appreciated that although this task will result in a variety of body shapes being assumed in the air, shape itself has not been stressed. At this stage it is incidental and the attention of the class is directed towards awareness and use of different body parts. (*See* Plate 8.)

In the early stages of flight the accent should be on resiliency, as children are, on the whole, naturally more concerned with producing a succession of actions such as skipping or hopping. They enjoy experimenting with parts of the body other than feet on which they can bounce, and are prepared to choose activities involving shins, hips and shoulders. Bouncing, combining body parts such as hands and feet, can also be explored by some.

Within the jumping action the body spends such a comparatively short time in the air that the landing often occurs before any specific preparation or conscious effort can be made. In the transference of weight on to hands and feet, as in repetitive crouch jumps, the feet, which are usually both the ejectors and receivers of weight, are allowed more time in the air to prepare for the landing; consequently attention can be paid to meeting the floor. This "slow motion" effect of landing, for some, will be the experience they will find most valuable when considering the landing action. Weight should be received on to two feet or the feet used one after the other on landing, assuring equal efficiency in both methods of landing. As children become more proficient in flight and able to combine a variety of ways of transferring weight, *e.g.* run, jump, land and roll, they can be expected to produce appropriate ways of landing.

It is in the first two years with Juniors or the first year in the Secondary school that children should become thoroughly familiar with and skilful in ways of using the feet in take-off and landing. They should also have been given guidance in efficient ways of landing so that they feel confident in jumping from a variety of heights. Although the principles of landing are common to all, the teacher should be particularly aware of children who, through habit, lack of control or fear, land awkwardly. These individuals are always liable to have accidents, particularly as the flight becomes varied. Some children land with the feet wide apart, which could lead to damage to the knee. Others land with one or both feet slightly inturned, making ankle and knee liable to injury. A few children tend to assist landing on the feet with one or both hands, probably a continuation of young children's liking for landing on all fours. This could be dangerous, particularly when the weight is not directly over the feet and the hands are placed in front or behind in a misguided attempt to counteract the natural momentum and direction of the falling body. It is very difficult to break such habit actions so the teacher must deal with them promptly, before they become well established. These children need individual help and constant reminding of what they must do to correct such faults whenever landings occur in a lesson.

It is only by steering the children progressively through these early stages that the confidence required for the more advanced work will be gained and a real enjoyment of flight becomes possible.

This chapter covers only the elementary aspects of flight as a means of transferring weight; the three phases—take-off, period in the air and landing—are dealt with in greater detail in Chapter 14.

Although the teacher will guide his class through all the methods of transferring weight, only in the very early stages will these actions be performed in isolation. As soon as he feels the class capable of managing the body safely using one method, two ways of transferring weight at least should be combined. If, as previously suggested, rocking and rolling, and flight and sliding are introduced simultaneously, then choosing other appropriate ways is a natural progression.

With more experienced children the teacher should aim to foster the ability to build sequences, selected from the variety discovered, and to perform any combination of actions fluently.

Apparatus

Work on apparatus challenges the children to perform types of action experienced on the floor at a variety of levels and on different surfaces, and to choose the appropriate method of transference of weight, so that movement over the apparatus becomes a logical and efficient way of travelling.

With Juniors just beginning this work, each method of weight transference should be explored separately. Apparatus should be provided where sliding, for example, is the activity which is emphasised, and although in order to slide down they must first climb up, sliding is the main action with which the teacher helps them to experiment. Climbing apparatus such as rope ladders, scrambling nets or wallbars allows the group to explore step-like transferences of weight. Although the hands and feet are naturally used when climbing, the class should be encouraged to try gripping with other parts. Juniors will provide a great variety of answers to the problem of showing flight either on or off or over apparatus. The teacher should help by ensuring that the apparatus is not too high at first. Where this is impossible, an inclined approach could be provided. He can suggest various ways of approach and encourage the group to use a number of different body parts to bear weight while fulfilling the task.

The following tasks on apparatus could be given to a class who have just begun this work and need to experiment with each of the methods of transferring weight.

Apparatus—low table, or box top or form.
   Task.—Find different ways to get on and off or over.

Aparatus—two inclined forms on stools, with a linking bar.
   Task.—Experiment with different ways of sliding — up and down the inclined forms and along the bar either on top or underneath.

Apparatus—climbing frame.
   Task.—Climb up, travel along and climb down, showing weight bearing on at least three different body parts.

Apparatus—steps or stage blocks.
   Task.—Jump on and off or over.

Apparatus—mats.
   Task.—Free practice in rolling, showing variety.

Apparatus—a series of canes supported on skittles.
   Task.—Alternately jump over and slide or roll under.

When considering apparatus for actions involving the transference of weight, the teacher should bear in mind that the four methods of weight transference can seldom be considered in absolute isolation. The following headings therefore consider two of the more usual combinations. The linking of like actions as in rocking and rolling should be taught first, as the transition is comparatively simple. Later, other combinations which include joining unlike actions, involving change of level for example, as in flight and rolling, can be attempted.

ROCKING AND ROLLING

These two actions can be performed over a low bar, on forms or low box top. It may be found that to cover the bar with a mat will provide a more comfortable surface on which to rock. The children can find ways of rolling along a form, forwards and backwards. They can experiment, using feet on the floor astride the form while the trunk rolls along the form, and complete the whole action with the body at the same level. The possibilities and advantages of rocking into rolling can also be explored. This activity will involve the performer in skilfully balancing and controlling the body on the narrow surface provided by the form.

Apparatus—low box top, mats.

    Task 1.—Get on to the box, roll along the top and jump off. Cross the mat using a different type of roll.

    Task 2.—Get on to the box, roll along and off, and roll again on the mat.

    Task 3.—Go straight from the floor into a roll on the box, rock off into a roll.

In the first task the roll will be completed on the same level, whereas in the second and third either the take-off or the completion will be on a different level from the roll itself.

STEP-LIKE ACTIONS AND FLIGHT

Getting on to apparatus at first usually involves step-like transferences in order to gain height so that flight may follow.

Using fixed wall bars, window ladders and double bars or any kind of climbing apparatus, the tasks could be to climb up and jump down, or climb up, get through and jump down. The transferences here include negotiating comparatively small, vertical gaps. The children could also be expected to cover narrow, horizontal gaps where the level remains the same, *e.g.* two forms or two low box tops.

Apparatus such as the horse, box, buck or bar box can be used to get on using step-like transferences and get off by means of flight.

FLIGHT AND ROLLING

Rolling will have been practised at many of the earlier stages and can now be linked with landing from a jump. This necessitates an ability to move fluently from high to low level and involves a quick adjustment of body weight. It is, however, an essential skill and the class should be encouraged to explore with apparatus at a low height:

1. landing and rolling in the same direction as the body weight — this can be experienced jumping forwards, backwards, sideways and with the body turning;
2. landing and rocking;
3. landing, controlling the body weight and re-directing the body into a roll.

The first two methods are the more usual and children should learn to feel where the body weight is on landing and act accordingly. Occasionally it is impossible to follow the natural direction, because of obstacles in the pathway of the mover, and the performer may be forced to resort to the third method.

It will be obvious from the above examples that many other natural combinations of transferring weight can be used, such as sliding into rolling, and step-like transferences into sliding. Eventually the class should be able to combine three or even all methods when using apparatus, if this has been arranged thoughtfully and with the theme in mind. The following examples could be used with children who have already been introduced to this movement idea and have experimented as suggested above.

Apparatus—an inclined form to a hinged side wall and a mat.
  Task.—Starting point A: a sliding action up the form; get through, along and jump down, roll over the mat. Starting point B: roll over the mat, climb up, travel along, get through and slide down.

Apparatus—bar box, two forms, two mats.
  Task.—A, B and C show possible starting points. Take any starting point and using at least three pieces of apparatus show three different methods of transferring weight.

Apparatus—horse and two mats.

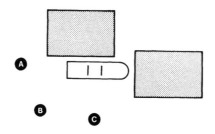

Task.—A, B and C are possible starting points. Approach from any angle, arrive on different body parts and get off using step-like actions; roll over mats.

Apparatus—a form inclined to a wall bar, two mats.

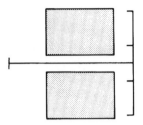

> *Task.*—Use the apparatus and include at least three ways of transferring weight.

Apparatus—a high bar and mats.

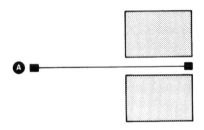

> *Task.*—Starting point A. Travel along the bar (on top or underneath), using step-like and sliding actions, use flight to get off and a roll on the mat.

Apparatus—box, medium height.
> *Task.*—Approach from any angle using a step-like transference to get on, and flight to get off.

Apparatus—low box and mattress.
> *Task.*—Run, jump on to and off or over the box, land and roll.

Apparatus—horse, box and two mats.

Task.—Include three ways of transferring weight within a sequence, using all the apparatus.

CHAPTER 6

Intermediate Body Management

Themes covered in the preceding chapter have stressed travelling and stopping, and the attention has been focused on specific body parts in action. In intermediate body management, however, the attention shifts to considerations of stretching and curling, twisting and turning and symmetry and asymmetry where the concern is with the body as a whole and locomotion and stillness become incidental.

STRETCHING AND CURLING

Material

When children are aware of the variety of travelling possibilities and have become familiar with ways of taking weight and transferring weight, the changing shape of the body whilst it is moving can be explored. The comparatively simple actions of curling and stretching will have been performed already many times, but the attention may well have been directed towards other problems.

Flexion and extension are integral parts of any action and common to all movement. Curling and stretching are movements which are possible because of the flexible structure of the spine and both are related to a centre, which in whole body movement would be the centre of the body. Stress differs, however, in that in curling it is to close around this area whilst in stretching the main aim is to reach out and away from it. In some instances, however, the pull away will be related to the base in addition to a centre as such. The stretching of the body when lying or standing in an elongated position will be equally stressed in both the upper and lower halves, away from the central region, whereas the stretch experienced in a handstand will be felt as a pushing away from hands or base, although the feeling of reaching away from the centre should remain. Stretching can also be experienced with the limbs spread, emphasising breadth, as in a cartwheel.

Hyperextension of the spine results in the body arching, and this can produce backward or lateral movements with one half of the body stretching while the other naturally compensates by contracting. In backward arching the front surface is extended while the back contracts, whereas when the sideways arch is achieved, it is one side of the body which is stretched while the other becomes compressed.

Teaching

In all the previous ways of moving the body will have alternated between these two actions. Reference will have been made many times to both curling and stretching when rocking and rolling, while stretching will probably have been encouraged when dealing with certain aspects of flight. For a brief period it may be found valuable for children to experience the two extremes possible within this movement idea, in positions of stillness. Having to concentrate on rounding and elongating the spine and feeling its resulting effect on the whole body is useful as these two activities are obviously initiated in the trunk and awareness of this area is often neglected. Children should be guided towards feeling the positions of curled and stretched and also the process of *becoming* curled and stretched, appreciating the difference between "I am *stretched*" and "I am *stretching*".

If stretched and curled positions are achieved as the natural conclusion of stretching or curling actions, they can be of value in experiencing the ultimate. If children are merely expected to produce isolated stretched or curled positions the results will be relatively useless. It is the interplay and compensatory reactions of the body moving into and between curled and stretched positions that should be experienced. *Static positions unrelated to each other are of little value, but the feeling of stretching and the differing sensation experienced in curling, and moving from one to the other, are the important factors to be considered.* Some of the justifiable criticisms levelled against the results of lessons with this theme as their focus might well be avoided if teachers were to recognise the full implications of the previous sentence.

It should be realised at this juncture that in the action of stretching the body can be elongated, stressing the upper and lower halves reaching in opposite directions, or it can be wide, accentuating the right and left sides pulling away from the central line, the spine. In the very early stages of stretching or curling the trunk should be made the most important part of the body, as children readily achieve extension and flexion in the limbs but find mobility of the trunk a much more difficult task. The head, too, should be included in both these actions whether it is regarded as part of the trunk and an extension of the spine, or looked upon as another limb.

When children are being led through these first experiences it is probably better for the teacher to suggest parts of the body which might take weight. It should be realised that only in positions of lying, standing on either toes or hands, and in the air, can a complete stretch be made, while curled positions can occur on feet, shins, either side and any part of the back. The whole class could quite quickly explore most of these possibilities, the majority being capable of experiencing all.

Having felt the extremes of curling and stretching with the body supported on bases selected by the teacher, the children can now experiment with other bases, symmetrical and asymmetrical, over which the rest of the body can extend or curl. It will be found that only an incomplete stretch is possible once the weight is taken on the shoulders or certain other parts of the body. Even so, when these bases are used the teacher should stress that the parts free and capable of stretching should do so to the full. Similarly, in curling it will be discovered that on certain bases one part of necessity will need to be extended, although the majority of body parts will be able to curl over this base.

The ability of the spine to curve and arch backwards, forwards and laterally must be exploited if true versatility and mobility are to be achieved. Often curling results only in forward and backward rolling actions, whereas if children are encouraged to experiment with the idea that the spine is capable of arching backwards and sideways, not only will a greater variety of ideas result but also a more skilful response will be demanded.

Most of this work will have been achieved statically and soon travelling should be stressed, as this necessitates weight being taken on various body parts, which will help the performer to experience leading into, moving through and resolving actions where the body is stretched or curled. The relation and interdependence of the two actions will also need to be understood: that in order to extend, a preparatory flexion is required, and that the natural reaction after a complete stretch is for the body to recover by contracting.

Travelling will probably include flight and it is here that the teacher should realise the difficulties involved in curling when airborne. It is much simpler to stretch in the air as, after take-off and in preparation for landing, the legs are already extended, while in an upward thrust the upper half of the body is automatically affected in the attempt to overcome gravity. Thus the reaction of the body would seem to tend towards extension in the air and all the ways of stretching should be explored first before experimenting with curling the body in flight. Most children will find this difficult to achieve, as it involves a complete action taking place after take-off and before meeting the floor, and a deterioration in landing might result. It may be that the teacher will prefer to postpone this stage and deal with it later in advanced flight.

Apparatus

In the planning of apparatus for this theme the normal ways of using the body should be considered, *i.e.* flexion usually both precedes and follows extension, the actions of curling and stretching thus alternating. It would be pointless to expect children to travel over several pieces of apparatus maintaining either a curled or stretched position, but the teacher should guide them to explore the many possibilities of stretching and curling according to the situations presented. It will soon be realised that in an action where the body is first curled and then extended, parts of the body may be stretched while others remain tucked. For example, one part may be gripping the apparatus while the freed part reaches out to receive weight, as when swinging on a rope where the arms are flexed and the legs prepare to land, or when climbing a rope where the upper and lower limbs work alternately gripping, reaching, pulling and pushing.

Young children can work with raised canes or hoops, individual mats and skipping ropes on the floor or forms and large mats, before introducing work on larger pieces of apparatus.

Apparatus—two individual mats.

> *Task.*—Cross A keeping the body curled, cross B stretching. Find your own way of joining the two movements.

Apparatus—two individual mats and two skipping ropes.

> *Task.*—Travel across the mats keeping the body curled, travel over the ropes going from side to side with weight on hands and the rest of the body alternately stretching and curling.

Apparatus—raised canes and hoops.
> *Task.*—Travel in, out and over, stretching and curling.

Forms and mats can be used with either beginners or more experienced classes.

Apparatus—a form used broadways.
> *Task.*—Travel across the form keeping the body tucked and return showing a stretch or arch.

Apparatus—a form used lengthways and a mat.
> *Task.*—Travel along the form alternately stretching and curling. Jump off the end and roll over the mat.

Tasks can also be given using individual pieces of apparatus.

Apparatus—a bar at hanging height.
> *Task.*—Travel along either stretching or alternately stretching and curling.

Apparatus—a low bar.
> *Task.*—Travel along jumping over and returning by rolling over or under.

Apparatus—ropes.
> *Task 1.*—Travel up. (This will probably involve alternate stretching and curling.)
> *Task 2.*—Using one or two ropes explore the possibilities of changing shape whilst the ropes are still or moving.

Apparatus—climbing frame, window ladders or double bars.
> *Task.*—Travel up and down, over or across with the body alternately stretching and curling.

Apparatus—box top or two layers of the box and mats.
> *Task.*—Arrive on using hands and feet; get off with hands touching the mat first. (This task will result in the body curling on arrival and stretching to get off.)

Apparatus—horse and mats; starting points A and B.

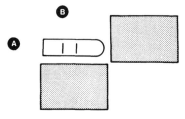

> *Task.*—Arrive on and get off by taking weight on hands and achieving a stretch to land. Roll over either of the mats.

When children have had sufficient time to experiment on single pieces of apparatus, they can be presented with a more complicated arrangement where they explore curling and stretching possibilities before selecting a series of actions to be the basis of a sequence.

Apparatus—two forms, a buck and two mats.

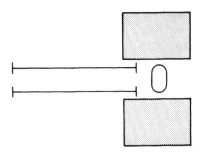

Apparatus—one form, two ropes and a box.

Apparatus—two bars, two inclined forms on the lower bar, two saddles and two mats.

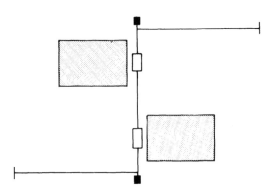

Apparatus—inclined form to a bar box, a horse with one pommel, two mats.

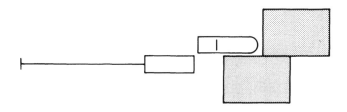

TWISTING AND TURNING

Material

Two further actions of which the body is capable are those of twisting and turning. Twisting is made possible because of the jointed nature of the body and if increased mobility is to be achieved then the variety of additional gymnastic actions which result from work on this theme needs to be thoroughly explored and the principles understood.

Twisting occurs when one body part is stabilised and the rest of the body screwed so that different surfaces face different fronts, *i.e.* parts of the body act in opposition producing torsion. Variety within the action of twisting is possible once the principle is established. The body may be kept compact and near the fixed part or it may reach away from the supporting area, thus providing opportunities for both curling and stretching while twisting.

A twist may be resolved either by releasing the fixed part, in which case turning usually results, or, once the twist has reached such a state that it can go no further, by allowing the body to recoil, the inherent speed changes involved in twisting becoming apparent. It will be found that movements leading into twisting are usually performed comparatively slowly, decreasing as the ultimate twisted state is reached, whereas the recoil will be explosive, with the initial burst of speed decreasing as the body returns to normal.

Different parts can be used to initiate a twisting action although eventually the whole body becomes involved.

Often the part leading the body into a twist is the part that eventually takes and maintains weight. An effective way of preparing for a twisting action is to screw the body in the opposite direction first, when the release of tension will result in added impetus to the main action.

Turning concerns the body as a whole rotating at right angles about one of three possible axes — the up-down or vertical axis, and the two horizontal axes, the side to side and the forward-backward. Actions resulting from the body revolving around the vertical axis are those such as rolling with the body maintaining an elongated position, spinning on the hips, turning jumps, or making quarter or half turns from a balance on hands. Forward and backward rolls are examples of the body rotating round the side to side axis, while moving through an inverted balance into an arch is an instance where the revolution is only half completed. A cartwheel will be recognised as an action where the rotation of the body is around the forward-backward axis. Angular flight, that is flight involving rotation, can be achieved not only in turning jumps about the vertical axis, rotation can occur around all three axes and result, for example, in aerial somersaults or can involve rotation about two axes when twists are incorporated. (*See* Plates 9 and 10 and Plates 33 —37.)

PLATE 9

PLATE 10

Pivoting, swivelling and spinning are actions which involve turning and can be seen as similar in some respects to sliding. Pivoting suggests that impetus is recharged intermittently by a further action of a body part other than that taking the main weight. Swivelling or spinning occur when the initial action only is used to maintain the motion, which will eventually lose momentum and come to an end. The speed of the body can be varied to some extent in all these actions by the shape it assumes while rotating — a compact body will revolve at greater speed than when the body is spread. The surface areas used in pivoting, swivelling and spinning can be the same as in sliding. The flow of the movement in all sliding actions, whether on the spot or travelling, may be less bound than in many other gymnastic activities and provide moments when comparative free flow can be experienced and enjoyed.

Whereas turning is concerned with the body as a whole, twisting involves awareness of parts within the whole acting against each other. The fact that the body moves as a unit in turning permits simultaneous action only, whereas in twisting body parts are used successively, joints coming into action one after the other.

Unless use is made of twisting and turning actions the performer is limited to movement in the forward-backward and up-down directions. Twisting in isolation can result in static contorted positions being achieved with no further aim in view, but if the ability of the body to twist is exploited gymnastically then the action becomes purposeful.

In curling, stretching, twisting and turning the body is used to the fullest extent and if versatility is to be fostered all must be explored in depth. The ability to move fluently and with awareness, using these four actions appropriately both on the floor and on apparatus, is not easy to achieve, but when developed provides the performer with a very much wider range of activity.

Teaching

As with curling and stretching, if the teacher directs the initial experiences he can ensure that each child understands some of the fundamental principles involved within the action.

There is little point in twisting into a position only to resolve it along the same pathway, and teachers should ensure from the outset that a twist is used functionally in so far as it can be used, for example, to:

change direction,

transfer weight, or

gain initial impetus for a turning action.

The following tasks place children in situations where the body twist is resolved with the focus on transference of weight.

> *Task* 1.—Start in a crouch position with weight on the feet, which are kept fixed. Use the hands to walk round the base until a position is reached where they can go no farther. Take weight on to the hands, release the feet and ground them again in a different place. (The teacher should ensure that twisting to both right and left is explored. A progression then is for the hands to be placed as far behind the body as possible and the twist resolved in the same way.)

Task 2.—Begin with weight on the shoulders with the legs extended symmetrically above the base.   Draw both knees down over either the right or left shoulder and transfer weight, ending in a kneeling position.

Task 3.—Take up a kneeling position and place one hand on the floor.   Allow the other hand to lead the body into the space between the fixed hand and the knees. Transfer weight on to one shoulder and either roll or maintain the weight over this base.

The class could now be given the task of discovering new ways of transferring weight from feet to hands and, by twisting, bringing the feet down in a different place. Here each child will solve the task in his own way and results may range from asymmetrical crouch jumps to variations of handstands and cartwheels with twists.   Using their previous experience of rocking, some could now experiment with ways of twisting out of front rocking, where it will be discovered that if a quick twist is used either at the beginning or end of the action, weight can be transferred on to the back. The twist will occur when the weight is on the upper half of the body and the lower half is free to twist against it or vice versa.

Twisting can be combined with curling or stretching, when the body screws downwards towards the supporting base or the part which is eventually to take weight reaches away from the support.

In turning the possibilities are varied but actions such as rolling will have already been experienced. This leaves only wheeling, spinning and aerial rotation as new activities to be explored.   The former is limited to actions where weight is borne alternately on the hands and feet with the body wheeling over successive supports and children should be given a brief experience of this way of turning. The resulting actions will develop, for some, into cartwheeling, for others, into unnamed wheeling skills.   Spinning, swivelling and pivoting on different parts of the body can be explored, with the children being encouraged to use twisting as a preparation for these activities. Angular flight about the horizontal axis and flight involving both twisting and turning may be achieved only by the more able performers who attend the school gymnastic club or classes organised by other bodies. Nevertheless those who are capable of producing, for example, aerial somersaults, cartwheels or walkovers should be encouraged to practise and perfect these skills and include them, when appropriate, in sequential work.

Twisting and turning are easily linked as one often either precedes or results from the other. The opportunity to explore all the possibilities offered by both in gymnastics results eventually in the body being used in a skilful and versatile way.

Further aspects of twisting and turning are dealt with in Chapter 14 on Flight.

Apparatus

Children need to be reasonably competent before this theme is introduced since the changes of orientation which have to be accommodated while the body twists and turns on apparatus should not be underestimated. Apparatus nevertheless adds a new dimension to this theme in that, unlike the floor, it provides gripping surfaces; a fact which will readily stimulate a variety of response. (*See* Plates 11, 12, 13 and 14.)

PLATE 11

PLATE 12   PLATE 13

PLATE 14

Apparatus—mats and forms.

> *Task* 1.—Grip the form and by releasing the lower limbs bring about a twist and a change of direction; on landing fix the feet and allow the upper half to initiate the twist and take the body weight. Repeat this travelling along the form.
>
> *Task* 2.—Experiment with fixing other body parts on the apparatus and bring about twisting.

The teacher can, if necessary, suggest parts of the body to fix and encourage the use of the different levels provided by the form and the floor.

Apparatus—junior frames, wallbars both hinged and fixed, window ladders and single and double bars.

> *Task* 1.—Experiment with fixing parts of the body by means of gripping, *e.g.* parts of the foot, the back of the knee, the front of the hips, and waist.

Task 2.—Travel up and down, along or across with a repetitive twisting action.

Task 3.—Experiment with a variety of ways of rolling around the bars; include rotation around the three axes.

Apparatus—ropes.

Task 1.—Experiment turning the body both forwards and backwards between two ropes.

Task 2.—Swing on one rope, twisting and turning at the end of the action. (This will necessitate an active use of the lower half of the body.)

Individuals will invent their own methods of using one or two ropes to bring about twisting providing they have understood the principles involved. (*See* Plate 15.)

PLATE 15

Apparatus—horse, saddles, box and buck, used singly.

　　Task 1.—Find ways of getting on and off showing a change of direction. (This will involve either a turn or a twist.)

　　Task 2.—Get on and find ways of getting off so that the body finishes facing the apparatus. (This also, in most cases, will bring about either a twist or a turn.)

　　Task 3.—Get on and jump off and roll, at some point bring about a twist.

When setting out more complicated apparatus it will help if the apparatus is placed initially at angles other than ninety degrees.

Apparatus—form angled to a horse and a mat.

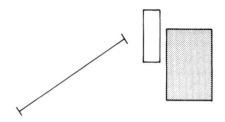

Apparatus—form angled to a box and a mat.

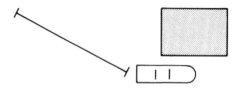

Apparatus—form angled to a bar box, ropes and a mat.

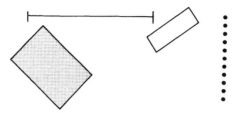

Apparatus—a low bar, one form inclined and one on the floor, two saddles and two mats.

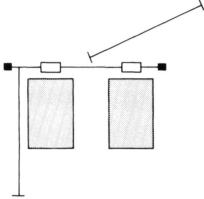

Apparatus—a bar at medium height, three forms, one underneath the bar, one inclined and one on the floor, two mats.

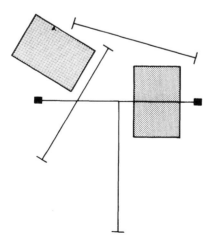

Apparatus—a form angled to the buck and a mat.

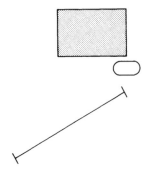

Tasks on such apparatus could be to use twisting and/or turning actions:

    (a) to negotiate corners,
    (b) to bring about changes of direction while travelling,
    (c) to initiate a change of level.

SYMMETRY AND ASYMMETRY

Material

Symmetry can be defined as equal proportions of the whole being distributed on either side of a line or plane into two or more parts exactly similar in size, shape and in position relative to the dividing points. The term bilateral symmetry is used when reference is made to the structure of the body; the balance of parts being equal on either side, with the limbs arranged matching and in opposition in relation to the central dividing line of the vertebral column.

Although the body itself is symmetrical, the majority of actions are performed asymmetrically. Eating, writing, walking are asymmetrical activities, where one side only is stressed or where the sides are used alternately. Rarely does one sit, stand or lie symmetrically although unlike writing and walking this is a possibility.

Symmetrical movement in gymnastics demands discipline, control, co-ordination and a keen sense of body awareness. Symmetrical locomotion is limited to the forward-backward direction and movements up and down, as any deviation from these leads into actions with a one-sided stress. In asymmetrical actions one side of the body becomes more active or a greater stress is laid on the right or left. This brings about uneven, lopsided actions where the body has to adapt to unequal and irregular stresses and all manner of twists and turns and changes of direction become possible. Twisting and turning are related to each other and both are associated with asymmetry. Turning about the side to side axis, however, is the only method of rotation where symmetrical or asymmetrical movement is possible. Turning about the up-down and forward-backward axis, where the body is divided into right and left sides will, of necessity, require one side to lead and an asymmetrical action will result.

Experience of both symmetrical and asymmetrical ways of moving are valuable in that each makes a particular demand upon the performer. Moving symmetrically requires skill and an ability to manage the body in a stable, balanced way, where a feeling of precision and poise can be experienced. A greater variety of action is possible within asymmetrical movements, giving the inventive performer an opportunity to experience the one-sided stress and to master completely new skills involving uneven distribution of weight.

Teaching

This theme is rather more advanced than those previously taken, so that in the beginning it is dealt with in a very elementary way. Perhaps with young children the words themselves may not even be mentioned, other words such as "matching", "balanced", "even", "level", "lopsided", "odd" and "uneven" can be substituted. It will be found useful, however, to have covered the first stages of this concept before attempting more advanced work, as many progressions depend upon the performer being able to manage his body in both symmetrical and asymmetrical situations and to appreciate the relationship between this idea and twisting and turning, for example, or gaining and terminating balance.

Initially each child can experience the symmetry of his own body by standing with weight equally distributed over both feet, appreciating the spine as the dividing line, the head being considered here as an extension of the spine, with the rest of the body matching on either side. Children can then be helped to explore other ways of achieving symmetry using a variety of bases. Within this task the body can be stretched, spread, rounded and arched. Symmetrical ways of travelling will be found and the limitations realised, among them that a double take-off only is possible and that the body is restricted to the forward and backward direction and movements up and down. For many this will mean that balances on hands and head, and backward rolls previously achieved with a one-sided stress, must now be mastered in a new way, presenting a challenging situation to the more able.

Asymmetrical use of the body is easier to appreciate once the precision of symmetry has been experienced, the children realising that the former provides a much greater freedom of action. The teacher should be careful here to see that asymmetrical actions are always purposeful. For example, posing on the shoulders with one leg stretched and the other bent is of little value, unless either the latter is being prepared to take weight in a backward movement or the body is going to be brought on to the feet and an asymmetrical placing is required for the following action.

It is essential that children experience the unusual adjustments which have to be made as a result of asymmetrical bases. Skilful redistribution of weight above sloping or irregular bases makes new demands even on the more able gymnasts, and it is this aspect which should be emphasised.

Often classes are found experimenting with the asymmetrical placement of limbs above a very stable symmetrical base; an undemanding task which makes no reference to the interesting and skilful shifts and adjustments of weight which should be resulting from work on this theme.

Even greater demands can be made if moving both symmetrically and asymmetrically is linked. The skill involved in familiar actions such as handstands and cartwheels can be extended by introducing such ideas as the following:

(a) lead into and out of a handstand asymmetrically but achieve symmetry at the point of balance;

(b) lead into a handstand symmetrically and resolve it asymmetrically;

(c) perform the whole action symmetrically;
(d) interrupt a cartwheel midway and achieve symmetry
      either complete the action normally
      or maintain symmetry to land.

This theme is valuable in that clarity, precision and a heightened sense of body awareness are required and, although some will find symmetrical actions difficult to master, the discipline and control demanded lead both to improved skill and to a more discriminating appreciation of line.

Apparatus

In Olympic gymnastics many of the vaults are symmetrical, necessitating double take-offs and two-foot landings. The apparatus itself is usually placed symmetrically and in most cases the body follows a straight line in a forward direction.

In sequential work, however, a blending of symmetry and asymmetry is encouraged to produce added variety and a more skilful use of the body when moving over apparatus.

Symmetrical actions on apparatus, as on the floor, are limited in number but require added control, balance and body awareness when working at the different levels provided by the apparatus. The possibilities of producing asymmetrical actions are greatly increased once apparatus is introduced as the variations in height of gripping surfaces can be exploited.

In the first few lessons on this theme with beginners it will be sufficient for the children to appreciate that the hands and feet can be used symmetrically and asymmetrically and they can experiment with ways of travelling along, up and down and over apparatus using one foot or two feet, one hand or two hands and also explore the possibilities of combining the symmetrical use of hands and asymmetrical use of feet, and vice versa. The task of travelling using two hands and two feet symmetrically along a form will probably but not necessarily result in the rest of the body moving symmetrically. In such cases the teacher could point out that in these actions not only do the limbs work symmetrically but the whole body travels with both sides matching. The class can then be given various pieces of apparatus to use such as climbing frames, ladders, planks, forms, steps, low box tops or stage blocks and challenged to travel symmetrically.

This method of moving on apparatus may be restricting for Juniors and so should not be pursued for long. The majority will probably grasp the main idea quite quickly and show both symmetrical and asymmetrical ways of travelling.

Provided that adequate time has been allowed for exploration at floor level the work on apparatus can progress very quickly at a later stage. Tasks on forms can be given which will guide the class towards appreciating that an asymmetrical base is inevitable when using the two levels.

Apparatus—form used broadside uppermost.
> *Task* 1.—Travel along placing the hands symmetrically on the form. (There is no need for the rest of the body to be symmetrical yet.)
> *Task* 2.—Travel across and back again using hands symmetrically on the form.
> *Task* 3.—Travel along and across using alternate hands to take weight.
> *Task* 4.—Travel along or across placing hands asymmetrically.
> *Task* 5.—Travel along or across placing one hand on the form and one on the floor.

Rolling symmetrically along forms forwards and backwards can be attempted. In some cases it will be found easier to achieve symmetry rolling along forms than on the floor, particularly if the feet and the trunk are at different levels.

Apparatus—form narrow side uppermost. (It will now be impossible to grip the form using the hands symmetrically unless it is approached at right angles. Therefore all but the first of the above tasks can be repeated.)

Apparatus—mats.
> *Task* 1.—Cross the mat symmetrically and recross asymmetrically.
> *Task* 2.—Work out an asymmetrical balance sequence.
> *Task* 3.—Travel around the edge of the mat using symmetrical movements, progress forwards and backwards, and negotiate the corners asymmetrically.

Task 4.—Approach the mat, cross and move away with matching and asymmetrical actions.

Apparatus—forms and mats.

Task 1.—Use both pieces of apparatus, showing symmetrical movements on one, asymmetrical on the other.

Task 2.—Using the form and mat together, achieve asymmetrical balance positions.

Task 3.—Jump over the form or use it to gain height. Gain symmetrical and asymmetrical body shapes in the air.

Apparatus—bar, hip height.

Task 1.—Cross the bar asymmetrically, recross symmetrically.

Task 2.—Cross asymmetrically, get under symmetrically.

Task 3.—Travel from one end to the other with asymmetrical movements on the bar and symmetrical movements on the floor.

Apparatus—double bars, low and medium height.

Task 1.—Travel up, over and down with a one-sided stress.

Task 2.—Use one bar to show symmetrical actions and the other asymmetrical actions.

Task 3.—Travel along using both bars together with a one-sided stress; develop a rhythmical phrasing.

Apparatus—climbing frames.

Task 1.—Travel up showing symmetrical movements, through and down with asymmetrical movements.

Task 2.—Invent a sequence travelling symmetrically and asymmetrically alternately.

When planning apparatus the placement can do much to suggest the appropriate use of symmetrical or asymmetrical actions. Apparatus set in a straight line will probably lead to a predominance of symmetrical movements, particularly if the task is to keep on the apparatus. Skilled performers might, however, easily produce a completely asymmetrical sequence. Apparatus placed at a variety of angles and offering different levels will help the beginner to travel asymmetrically.

Apparatus—a low box with four mats.

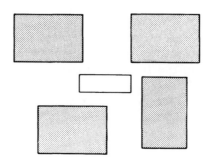

> *Task.*—Arrive from a variety of angles, change direction to get off. Get on and off taking weight on hands, stressing symmetrical and asymmetrical use of hands and feet.

Apparatus—two forms leading up to saddles on a low bar and two mats. The apparatus is duplicated so that six or more children can be divided into two groups.

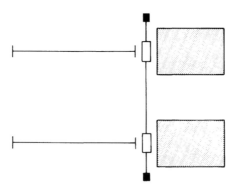

> *Task.*—Using all the apparatus, including a return activity over the bar. Stress symmetry but achieve asymmetry at least once.

Apparatus—a set of ropes, mattress and two forms.

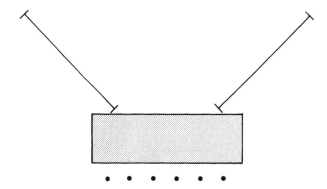

Task.—Take any starting point and, using all the apparatus, stress asymmetry.

Apparatus—a form leading to a low box, a horse and two mats.

Task.—Starting at point A, use the form to show asymmetry and the low box to show symmetry; move either symmetrically or asymmetrically over the horse.

Apparatus—four ropes and a box.
Task.—Use assisted flight on to the box from any angle, transfer weight and achieve flight off the box. (Using two ropes often leads to symmetry, and one to asymmetry.)

Apparatus—two forms, one leading to a horse, the other angled, and two mats.

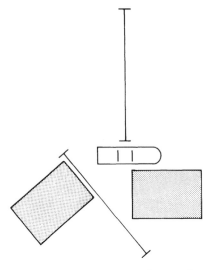

Task.—Use all the apparatus and negotiate the corners with asymmetrical actions.

This theme is ideal as an intermediate one as it links and develops work already covered yet demands greater skill, much care and thought.

If the elementary and intermediate themes are well taught the majority of children should reach a point when the more advanced work can be approached with confidence.

It should be stressed that the early stages must be thoroughly explored and sufficient time given to each idea so that interest, enjoyment, satisfaction, confidence and skill are all experienced before presenting the advanced themes.

CHAPTER 7

Control of Body Weight, Tension and Energy

Material

Skilful control is one of the most important aims in gymnastics. In order to achieve physical mastery the child must learn to manage his body weight and to produce the appropriate amount of tension and energy required in a variety of actions.

It is necessary to define some of the terms used in describing the body and the way in which it acts. The *kinesthetic sense* is the means by which changing muscular *tensions* are felt. The *weight* of the body is measurable and subject to the laws of gravity. The body produces *energy* which is the driving force for movement. All movement involves a degree of resistance, whether this is produced within the body itself or from without by people or by apparatus. Resistance is overcome by using measurable degrees of *strength*.

CONTROL OF WEIGHT

The control of body weight is one of the first considerations in gymnastics. The terms "weight bearing", "taking weight", "changing weight" and "transfering weight" suggest different movement considerations but they have in common the necessity to become aware of and manage the weight.

Since the body is subject to gravity it is usually necessary to resist this and resulting actions range from maintaining an upright position to actually ejecting the body into the air. An awareness of the pelvic region, where the centre of gravity is normally located, is vital in all situations where weight is being controlled.

Even in comparatively simple actions such as transferring weight from one base to another, management is important, particularly when the bases are far apart. The body weight must be held over the original base until it can be transferred onto the new base, otherwise falling or collapsing might result. Control in such situations can also be achieved by the trunk and free limbs leaning or pulling away from the part that is to bear weight, counteracting the tendency to topple over, until the new base is ready. In balancing actions the free limbs can be used to make fine adjustments so that the weight is controlled and retained over the base.

In actions such as swinging the weight is instrumental in bringing about change, impetus being gained and recharged by an active use of the body weight. Similarly, balance can be terminated by deliberately moving the centre of gravity so that it falls outside the base.

When a certain degree of control is attained and the body weight can be guided safely and used effectively, it is profitable to experiment with tipping, tilting or leaning actions. In these situations the weight can be shifted gradually so that, in order to avoid falling, locomotion takes place. If the weight is "let go" and caught again its role in stability and mobility can be recognised and exploited.

It is more difficult to control weight in the three phases of flight, that is, at take-off, while the body is in the air, and when it meets the floor again, than in situations where contact with the floor or apparatus is maintained.

CONTROL OF TENSION AND ENERGY

When muscular tension is present the body is active whether it is moving or holding a position. Lack of tension results in heaviness. The latter state taken to its extreme is the antithesis of movement and bodily control. Increasing tension produces gripping in the whole or parts of the body, while decreasing tension leads to relaxing.

In all gymnastic actions muscular tension is present but in some it is particularly important. When balancing the body is kept over the base and this implies that a certain degree of tension is produced. In holding a balanced position the body should have sufficient tension to maintain an upward stress rather than give way to a weighty, downward one. Actions concerned with a poised arrival on apparatus, especially from flight, involve changing degrees of tension. This enables the movement through space to be arrested and the body to achieve stillness, so that a balance can be maintained.

In gymnastics the floor provides the resistance against which the body pushes in order to lift or jump and to which the body adapts on landing.

In apparatus work where obstacles have to be mounted or cleared the energy expended is often considerable. For any type of jump to be effective there must be an outburst of energy. Similarly the release of a full twist, the slashing action of the legs to turn the body when swinging on a rope, the whipping action of the free limbs to cause loss of balance, the pressing of the hands against the floor or apparatus during inversion, are all characterised by the strength required for efficient performance.

Actions requiring less output of energy generally occur when the body is poised on apparatus, in some pinpoint balances, and while the body is the the air. However, in some flight situations it is evident that much energy is being expended as can be seen in the face of the gymnast in Plate 38.

The body must be involved as a unit when producing energy, whether the result is manifest in actions of the whole body or an isolated part. Because the hips are associated with the centre of gravity it is essential that the lower half of the body is used to maximum effect when strong actions are required. The upper half of the body, particularly the head and chest, become important in actions where the energy output is reduced.

An awareness of the changing tensions and the differing amounts of energy which the body can produce is vital to the gymnast. Without this awareness the work might be bodily competent but lacking in quality, vitality and interest. Indeed, one hallmark of a very able gymnast is the ability to make actions demanding much skill and energy appear effortless. This illusory aspect as when, for example, a skilled performer is seen to soar through the air to alight in a perfect inverted balance on high apparatus without any obvious output of energy would, it seems, qualify the act to be worthy of aesthetic consideration.

In gymnastics there is a certain association between the rate at which the body moves and the amount of energy expended. The most usual combination is seen in strong, quick actions. Inverting the body, getting off the ground and on to or over high apparatus usually necessitates a strong action which, in order to be effective, must be executed quickly. This combination of speed and energy gives to gymnastics its characteristic zest.

Teaching

All movement involves body weight and, to a greater or lesser degree, tension and energy. Therefore, this is not a theme to be taken over a series of lessons but should be an ever-present consideration of the teacher who leads the children progressively towards an understanding of the problems involved. The relevant aspects of weight, tension and energy are discussed in each specific theme but it is profitable to see how the teacher can develop these throughout the work as a whole.

In the elementary stages children are given varied experiences which are aimed at enlivening their kinesthetic sense. The awareness and control of the body weight is an intrinsic part of this fundamental work. Locomotion, stillness, weight bearing and weight transference are situations in which management of weight is the prime concern. Children's physical growth should always be taken into account; height, weight and proportions alter, so the teacher cannot expect that once control is gained at any particular stage it will remain. Because of this and the fact that new situations are presented as the work progresses, control of weight is an aspect of movement to which the teacher should refer frequently.

In curling, stretching, twisting and turning, children must feel the different tensions which are characteristic of these actions. The weaker tension and inward focus of curling should be contrasted with the two-way outward pull of stretching, the radiating tensions of spreading and the varying stretched and compressed tensions within twisting. The teacher must ensure that children experience these tensions often and to the full, for the particular tensional "feel" associated with an action should be remembered and retained, so that it becomes a part of the movement experience that can be reproduced accurately when required. Symmetry, asymmetry and body shape in stillness and when moving are also achieved by muscular tensions and the bodily "feel" is again important. When children can consider and control the changing tensions within their bodies their work becomes livelier and clarity of movement is possible.

Although output of energy has always to be considered in gymnastics the first time this is stressed is probably when flight is introduced as a way of transferring weight. In all jumping activities, particularly in bouncing, where resilient recoveries are important, considerable energy is needed. With young children, whose energy seems limitless in this respect, the teacher has an excellent opportunity to make certain that these activities are fully experienced so that they can be extended and built upon later.

In order to tackle the more advanced themes children must have acquired a degree of bodily mastery which includes control of weight and the ability to select appropriate tensions and output of energy. Management of weight and control of tension is necessary in moving slowly and in addition quick actions demand much energy. In helping children achieve continuity of action the teacher must realise that it is only when weight, tension and energy can be controlled and used effectively that a blending of adjacent actions becomes possible.

When children work with a partner or within a group they are often in a situation where they have to cope with the weight of others, and this entails producing comparatively great degrees of strength. In the advanced themes of balance or flight the teacher should appreciate that the former is more concerned with weight and tension while in the latter it is the energy involved that is stressed.

The resistance and firm base provided by the asphalt playground and the wooden floor are accepted but rarely used in a conscious manner. Just as apparatus can be considered as an extension of the floor, in this respect the floor should be used as a piece of apparatus. One way of developing sensitivity is to set "touch before contact" tasks. In these the body part about to receive weight briefly touches the floor or apparatus prior to being placed ready for weight bearing. Such tasks need not be pursued for any length of time since their purpose is to aid sensitivity and they are not an end in themselves.

The one type of apparatus in which the control of body weight, tension and energy is of prime importance is that aiding the "take-off" phase of flight. Beating boards, spring boards and trampettes all require considerable skill in their use if they are to be effective. The relevant teaching points are discussed in detail on pages 239-41 of Chapter 14.

CHAPTER 8

The Use of Space

Material

The individual's interest in space is twofold. Firstly, his attention can be focussed on the space immediately surrounding the body, which is within his reach by normal extension. Secondly, the space shared by others and confined only by the walls of the gymnasium or playground or broken and sectioned by apparatus, can be equally important.

In the following aspects of this theme the focus of attention is on *where* the body is moving. In gymnastics movement follows either a straight or roundabout *pathway*, and at any time during locomotion, the body can be moving in one of three *directions* and at one of three *levels*. The *shape of the body* in space is constantly changing and this can be considered in both locomotion and stillness.

1. PATHWAYS

Locomotion is one of the main concerns in gymnastics and although the first consideration is body stressed, the track made when travelling is inextricably linked. At floor level, pathways involving the general space are immediately dictated by obstacles in the way of the mover. These may be mobile or stationary; mobile in the case of others also working in the general space, stationary when the deviations in track necessitated by walls, railings, projections or apparatus are considered.

While travelling the body can move in a straight line, along straight lines producing angular floor patterns, or can swerve and twist following a circuitous route. The relation between straight pathways and the symmetrical use of the body can be appreciated as well as the connection between twisting, asymmetry and the resulting indirect tracks. The course followed over apparatus can also vary with special attention being paid to angles of approaching and leaving the apparatus.

The floor and air patterns resulting from travelling actions will usually be incidental, but a growing awareness and ability to move fluently should be stimulated, and the deliberate following of a variety of pathways encouraged.

2. DIRECTION

When considering direction the attention is focused on the space immediately surrounding the body into which a part or the whole is about to move. The main directions in which the body travels in gymnastics are forwards, backwards and sideways and these are closely linked with stability. Deliberately moving into a diagonal direction can be associated with certain aspects of flight and loss of balance where momentary instability is experienced.

A change of direction can be brought about in two ways. The body can move forward, backward and then sideways,

(a) with no change of front, or
(b) continuing along a straight path, each action linked by a turn or twist.

When studying the relationship between twisting, turning, symmetry, asymmetry and change of direction, certain links can be established.

Symmetrical travelling is limited to the *forward* and *backward* directions, while moving *asymmetrically* allows the body to perform actions in all directions including those to the *side* and along the *diagonal.*

Twisting brings about continuous *changes of direction. Turning* about the *vertical axis* allows a *change of front* to occur. *Turning* about the *side to side axis* limits the movement to a *forward and backward direction. Turning* about the *forward and backward axis* brings about actions to the *side.*

3. LEVEL

When changes of level are observed it is the body as a whole which must be studied. Actions which elevate take the body *high* into the space beyond the normal reach, while those which keep the body moving near the floor involve travelling at the *low* level. The *medium* level in gymnastics tends to be "moved through" rather than stressed.

4. BODY SHAPE

The shape the body makes while travelling or in stillness is, at times, incidental. An awarenesss of the body outline in space and consequent shape, however, can often help clarify actions.

When curling, stretching, arching and twisting occur it is the actions that are stressed, the shape of the body remaining of secondary importance. Once the action becomes part of the movement vocabulary, a progression can be recognised when the shape of the body assumes a greater importance and the attention of the performer can be directed towards the body contour. It is here that the arch achieved in a back-bend can be fully appreciated, the wide, extended star shape of the cartwheel more defined and the elongation of the body in a handstand perfected. This is the stage when definition of shape adds clarity of line to an action and a positive attitude towards the body shape in space can be adopted. It may well be that the noticeable increase in the number of girls wearing gymnastic leotards has had a significant influence on awareness of body outline and consciousness of alignment.

The difference between movements where the body shape is maintained throughout the action, as in cartwheels and rolls, and those where a specific shape is only momentarily achieved, as in a handstand, can be contrasted.

The shapes that the body can assume while airborne can be explored. It has already been stated that stretching is simpler than tucking, but both are possible. Twisting and turning where changes of direction and front occur can also be achieved if anticipated in the take-off.

Apparatus limits the space and provides barriers to get over, under, in and out, through and round. In manoeuvring the body the shape is constantly changing, always adapting to the new situations presented by the apparatus. Moving partners and mobile apparatus such as ropes can provide both novel and challenging situations in that the fine timing required to negotiate spaces which are continuously altering demands considerable skill.

Teaching

These themes are essential if children are to appreciate and become aware of themselves in relation to others or apparatus. It is also important if they are to become adept at judging heights and distances relative to the body. In both cases it can be seen as a vital safety factor when children are moving in the gymnasium or playground. The awareness of both personal and general space is necessary if these are to be exploited, variety achieved and the body used to its fullest extent.

1. PATHWAYS

When travelling on feet the natural reaction of young children is to move around the hall or playground following a circular track and moving in a forward direction. If, however, they begin facing one other person they can be given the task of running, dodging and swerving to avoid others. This starting position is one way of ensuring that individuals will be facing different directions and when travelling commences an avoiding action must immediately be taken. When other tasks have been answered involving locomotion, often a greater variety can be achieved if the attention is drawn to the floor patterns created. The teacher may dictate the track or the class may be left free to invent their own. The following patterns are but a few from which a selection can be made.

Young children enjoy the challenge of producing recognisable floor patterns while travelling. It should be noted that direction and level of work are unimportant at this stage: it is the pathway that is stressed.

Suggested tasks linking locomotion and track:

Task 1.—Travel on hands and feet making a zig-zag path.

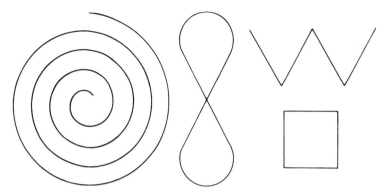

Task 2.—Travel on parts of the trunk creating a curved pathway.

Task 3.—Roll, making a circular track on the floor.

Older children could also work on this idea but it would not be necessary to dwell on pathways at floor level. The teacher could draw attention to the possibilities and refer incidentally to this when dealing with later themes and when working on apparatus. Air tracks could be explored with some classes, stressing the long, low trajectory required for length or the high, curving course needed if height is to be gained. Twists and turns while the body is upright in flight can be experienced by all, while actions where the body rotates in the air about other axes can be attempted by the few. Following a track made by a partner is fully covered in Chapter 11 on Partner Work.

2. DIRECTION

This aspect of space has an obvious link with the elementary body management themes and can be considered at any stage, when the main idea has been grasped. If, for example, a class has mastered travelling and stopping or pausing, an added challenge might be to change direction after each interruption.

When children have experimented with rolling actions, it would be sensible for the teacher to suggest that they attempt to roll in different directions.

It can be appreciated that the teacher needs to understand

the correlation between direction and the main theme being explored, and know the appropriate moment to make the connecting link for the children. It needs to be emphasised that a mere comment is not sufficient. The verbal noting, for example, that twisting brings about a change of direction, is of little value. This point must be translated into action, and the children allowed time to explore the idea anew, with this knowledge adding to their awareness of the movement possibilities.

The following tasks are examples of how the link can be made between directional changes and other themes.

> *Task* 1.—Starting on the feet, transfer the weight onto the shoulders.   Find three ways of answering this task, showing movement into different directions.
>
> *Task* 2.—Invent a sequence which includes stretching, arching and curling—each action must lead the body into a different direction.
>
> *Task* 3.—Using a variety of bases choose three actions which take the feet into the air. Bring about a change of direction by turning or twisting.
>
> *Task* 4.—Run, jump and turn in the air so that on landing a backward or sideways roll results.

3. LEVEL

Locomotion necessarily involves the body moving at one level or another, but when exploring this idea the stress is mainly on extending the normal range; getting as high or as low as possible and experiencing the transitions when moving easily through all three.

Young children enjoy pulling and pushing themselves along the floor, slithering and sliding, keeping very near to the ground. They delight in leaping and throwing themselves to the floor or launching themselves into space. They revel in space and need a sufficient area to experience this freedom.

Older children in general seem less inclined to exploit the space; few experience the exhilaration of true flight or enjoy moving very near to the ground.

The three phases of flight must therefore at this stage be handled carefully, and particular attention given to safe landings and efficient take-offs if confidence which may have been lost or undermined is to be restored. It is essential that children move fluently and without restraint at any level, and tasks involving leaping and rolling, including turning in the air and change of direction, springing on to the hands and dive rolls, should be given. The teacher must help children to move confidently from one level to another on the floor or forms before expecting work on this idea to be attempted on higher apparatus.

4. BODY SHAPE

The concern of the teacher should be to ensure that the facility with which actions are performed is such that the attention is no longer devoted entirely to the skill but can be directed also towards the shape of the body as it moves in space.

Attention can be drawn to body shape in a held position and clarity demanded

(a) at the beginning and end of a sequence,

(b) in a held balance, or

(c) by the individual providing an obstacle for a partner.

With older, more experienced classes, the teacher can expect a heightened awareness of the body in motion, on floor level and in flight. The changing body shapes in tucked jumps or catsprings, for example, can do much not only to clarify the action but also to help the performer master the skill.

Shape can readily be appreciated through observation of others and the teacher should take advantage of this by including short sessions in the introductory stages. Thus what is meant by shape can be seen, understood and implemented in the child's own work.

Apparatus

1. PATHWAYS

Pathways over apparatus are at first incidental to the actions performed but tracks become increasingly important as variety of approach and inventive use of apparatus are stressed.

Pathways can be influenced by the arrangement of apparatus—the two examples below suggesting the obvious, but not necessarily the only, pathway.

Apparatus—spring board, box, rope and mat.

Apparatus — form inclined to the bar box, horse and mat.

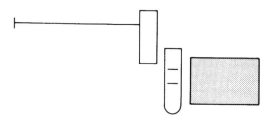

It should be noted that placement of spring boards, forms and mats particularly, does much to influence starting and finishing points.

A variety of track can be dictated by the teacher in the task set, although the placement of apparatus, as in the following example, suggests a straight line pathway.

Apparatus—form, low box, horse and mat.

Task.—Travel over the apparatus making a zig-zag track. (This will involve moving on and off or diagonally over the apparatus.)

A number of tracks should be possible in an arrangement so that individuals may choose their own, but the groups should be kept small so that, if desired, all may work at once. One example is given below of such an apparatus arrangement.

Apparatus—ropes, two bars, one form inclined to the high bar and the other flat, a spring board, box and horse.

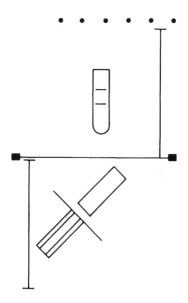

When stressing pathways attention should be drawn to spaces between apparatus and to the use of the floor in linking actions. If this point is not appreciated the continuity of action over apparatus is often interrupted and disjointed. At an early stage children should be encouraged to use floor space. Return activities utilising the floor can be suggested if apparatus is limited, *e.g.* when forms only are provided the challenge might include a floor task. With

younger classes small apparatus placed on the ground helps
to direct attention to possible paths, as in the following
examples.

Apparatus—a form and four individual mats.

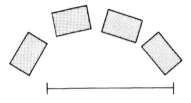

 Task.—Travel along the form making an angular path and
 travel over the mats using the curved track.

Apparatus—form and two skipping ropes.

 Task.—Travel along the form and return using either rope
 showing a clear change of path.

The air tracks can be highlighted when clearing apparatus,
by repetitive actions involving flight for example:

Apparatus—three forms placed at regular intervals and used
 broadways.
 Task.—Run and jump over or on and off each form producing repetitive air patterns.

A variation of this task could be to provide a situation where
both height and length are included.

Apparatus—two layers of the box leading to a high bar, the
 box so placed that flight is necessary onto the bar.

Task.—Run and use the box to leap on to the bar, swing and drop to the floor.

Air tracks can be stressed when swinging on ropes, where the pathway the body makes through the air can vary. If the body is taken into the air and released from the rope at the highest point, the air pattern is different from that made by the body if it swings into the air and is released only when the feet touch the floor at the lowest part of the swing.

Once this aspect of space has been dealt with it can be referred to whatever the main theme of the lesson. The teacher can expect the class to become increasingly aware of the variety of pathways possible on apparatus, and to select specific tracks relevant to the situation.

2. DIRECTION

The most natural way of travelling on apparatus is to move forwards and this must be taken into account when setting tasks which dictate direction. Apparatus which has to be mounted or cleared must of necessity be approached with the body moving forwards, but once in contact with the apparatus a change of direction can take place. Leaving the apparatus can equally well be effected moving backwards or sideways.

Apparatus such as bars, ropes and window ladders provide ample opportunity for moving in any direction, including the diagonal.

Flight into different directions can be experienced from forms, spring boards and trampettes and with the more skilled classes flight into the diagonal can be attempted.

Tasks on apparatus can ensure that the beginner experiences moving in to all directions.

Apparatus—three mats.

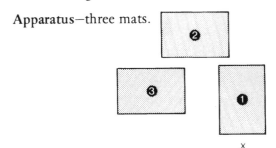

Task.—With X as the starting point, work over all three mats, forwards over mat 1, sideways over mat 2 and backwards over mat 3.

Apparatus—a form and mat.

Task.—Begin facing the form at X — cross and recross the form travelling forwards and backwards; move sideways over the mat.

Apparatus—box top, mat and form.

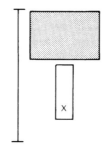

Task.—Starting at X move backwards over the box, sideways across the mat and forwards along the form.

Apparatus—spring board or trampette and mats.

Task.—Using the spring board or trampette, run, jump and land. At the first attempt land on mat 1 and from subsequent jumps land on 2, 3 and 4 in turn.

When children have explored the various possibilities of moving in different directions much more freedom can be given, for example:

Apparatus—high and low bar.
   Task.—Using each bar separately and at one point together include three changes of direction.

Apparatus—form, box, ropes and mattress.

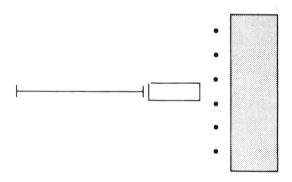

Task.—Start at the end of the form and travel to the mattress changing direction twice. (It would be possible to get diagonal flight on to the outer ropes from either end of the box.)

Apparatus—spring board, buck, ropes and mat.

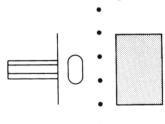

Task.—While travelling, bring about changes of direction by twisting and turning.

3. LEVEL

When apparatus is introduced, level becomes a dual consideration; the level on which the body is moving relative to the apparatus, and the height of the apparatus itself. Working in contact with apparatus which is at a height from the floor does not mean that the body is moving in the high area, although a feeling of being high may well be experienced.

Taking the body into the high level can be achieved by leaping onto, off or over steps, stage blocks, low tables or box tops, forms, spring boards and trampettes. Inclined forms or planks to stools, bar box or bar can be used once the class has the confidence to exploit these situations. Flight is more readily experienced leaving apparatus than when arriving but, if the task involves jumping from too great a height too soon, flight off may be inhibited since anticipation of landing will occur and rather than reaching into the space above the action will become one of dropping.

The ability to land resiliently from a height should be encouraged and the skill involved in moving easily from that position either into a roll or to rebound should be mastered.

In the following examples of tasks, the level is dictated, but whenever apparatus is being planned the teacher should keep in mind that level is an important factor.

Apparatus—hoop held parallel to the ground by a partner, or a cane raised on skittles.
    Task.—Run and leap high into or over the hoop or over the cane and return low by sliding or rolling underneath.

Apparatus—individual mats.
    Task.—Run and jump high over the mat, return keeping near to the ground.

Apparatus—form.
    Task.—Cross and recross alternately using the form to gain height and to keep low.

Apparatus—form and mats.

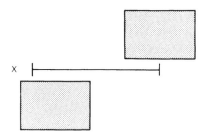

> *Task.*—Starting at X, move over the form and mats
> emphasising medium and low levels.

Apparatus—bar and mats; height of bar to be determined by
the height and ability of the group.
> *Task.*—Run and leap to grip the bar, land and roll across
> the mat.

Apparatus—inclined form on to a low bar and mat.
> *Task.*—Run and jump off the form, roll across the mat and
> return over the bar keeping the body near to the
> apparatus.

Apparatus—trampette, trapeze, high bar and mattress.
> *Task.*—Show changes of level while travelling over the
> apparatus.

Apparatus—two layers of the box, trampette, ropes and
mattress.

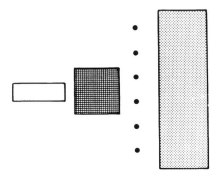

Task. —As above.

This arrangement offers greater scope for the more skilled performer since, unlike the previous example, it demands that the gymnast adapts to fluctuations in level. It can also be made progressively more difficult by

(a) raising the box,
(b) increasing the distances between box and trampette and trampette and ropes,
(c) encouraging diagonal flight from the trampette to the ropes not immediately ahead.

4. BODY SHAPE

This has to be taught with understanding otherwise static "poses" appear with the held shape bearing no relation to the arrival or method of leaving the apparatus. As in floor work the shape of the body can be considered in stillness or while travelling. Unlike work at ground level, however, the shape of the body is often dictated by the outline of the apparatus itself and by the spaces presented.

Children can more readily appreciate shape when the body remains in the normal upright position, and ropes, bars and wall bars provide situations where this is possible. It is a distinct progression when re-orientation in inversion is such that attention can be directed towards body shape. This stage can be reached more easily if teachers realise that some apparatus such as ropes, bars, window ladders and parallel ropes provides many points of support. These offer opportunities for the body to be held in or moved into the inverted position, affording a degree of security not always experienced on portable apparatus.

When balancing on apparatus has been mastered, the teacher could turn the attention of the more able children to the held shape. This not only provides a further challenge but also helps the performer achieve a greater clarity of movement resulting in more finished work.

Apparatus which assists take-off allows the performer a greater time in the air to achieve, establish and feel body positions. Ropes and bars are ideal apparatus upon which changing body shapes can be experienced while travelling.

A more advanced stage is reached when the performer is so competent while moving on and clearing apparatus that awareness of body line can be noted and appreciated.

Much of this work is for the skilled performer and those who are more spatially conscious than others although talented young children, particularly girls, are very capable of producing work which shows an acute and accurate appreciation of body alignment. Boys on the other hand are usually much more interested in acquiring skill; body line and finished work is often neglected, but for the advanced gymnast, work on this could produce a much higher standard of performance.

No specific tasks or arrangements of apparatus are given as this idea can develop from work already being produced on other themes such as weight bearing, balance or flight. It is for the teacher to recognise when an individual is capable of accepting the additional challenge and set tasks accordingly.

CHAPTER 9

Changes of Speed

Material

In the gymnastic themes considered so far the attention has been directed towards *what* the body is doing in any action. In this new movement idea the focus is on one aspect of *how* the action is being performed.

In order for movement to take place a degree of speed must be present, and in gymnastics it is the rate at which the body moves out of stillness through slow to fast which is explored. Both are easily distinguishable, with recognisable varying degrees between the two extremes.

Within most actions or series of actions, time changes are obvious, resulting in certain stresses, rhythms, accelerations and decelerations. Some gymnastic actions are, by their very nature, concerned with one element rather than the other. The speed inherent in the action of ejecting the body into the air, for example, is obvious; if a leap is to be effective then a quick, energetic use of the body is required. If, on the other hand, a balance is to be achieved, usually the point of equilibrium is reached by the body moving relatively slowly into position. Other actions can be performed at a variety of speeds depending upon the degree of proficiency already acquired. Activities such as rolling at different speeds can be attempted by the majority of children, although comparatively few will be able to perform cartwheels, for example, using more than one speed.

Within a single action time changes are often apparent; a handstand, for example, normally consists of a quick action to invert the body, a deceleration as the body becomes balanced over the hands and an acceleration as the feet return to the floor.

In the majority of sequences changes of speed become even more evident. When moving fluently from one action to another it is important to appreciate the appropriate use of speed and to acquire the ability to perform actions at a variety of speeds. This becomes increasingly important once apparatus is introduced for while at times a single action only is required, more often the challenge is such that the apparatus may be used more than once, or a sequence of movements performed using several pieces of equipment. This requires the performer to vary his speed over the apparatus, to blend recovery and preparation and to adapt his timing to the situations presented.

In gymnastics the tendency for individuals to move with a characteristic time stress is recognised. Although at first this is allowed to predominate the teacher should ensure that each child not only recognises the range possible within this theme but also is encouraged to extend his own. In this respect working with a partner is invaluable, since individuals are placed in the situation of moving with new time stresses, enlarging their speed vocabulary in the process.

When exploring the play between the two extremes of *quick* and *slow* it is natural to consider *acceleration* and *deceleration*. The ability to bring about an increase and decrease of speed quickly or gradually is an important safety factor in any gymnastic situation. It is also essential that the skill involved should be mastered, so that work on apparatus can be fully enjoyed and heights gained and distances covered with confidence. Acceleration or deceleration can best be experienced, in the first instance, by repetition of a single action, but can also be accomplished within a single action or within a sequence.

Both gaining and losing speed can produce highlights during a series of movements. A *climax* need not necessarily always be associated with quick, strong or elevated action but could be any moment which the performer wishes to stress, or when the main objective is achieved. This point may be reached once or several times and can occur anywhere within the sequence. When working at floor level the choice of accent is governed only by the task set, and the performer is comparatively free to choose the moments of climax.

Apparatus, however, not only dictates the accelerations and decelerations but also frequently influences the placing of accents.

Once the attention is drawn to the climax within a single action, or the most important action within a series, then the preparation for this moment and the ultimate recovery need to be considered. If the main action is to be effective then both preparation and recovery must be efficient. When these three phases are recognised the inherent *rhythms* within any sequence of movement can be studied, played with and enjoyed. It is important to realise that rhythm should develop naturally from the use of speed and energy appropriate to the action or sequence being performed. It should also be noted that although an increase in speed is usually associated with an increase in the output of energy this need not necessarily be so. Great strength and a considerable amount of energy are required in moving slowly into a difficult balance.

A rhythm can be established by repeating a single action which includes a time change. The rhythm can remain constant or can rhythmically accelerate or decelerate. Rhythm can also be stressed when performing two actions several times, or by accentuating the rhythmical timing within a sequence of varied movements.

Having dealt not only with *what* the body does but also *how* an action is performed, elementary movement ideas can be considered anew but with a different stress. The ability to control the speed at which the body moves can be investigated, *e.g.* in the themes of twisting and turning, and balance.

If the time changes normally associated with producing and releasing torsion are explored, it will be found that two possibilities present themselves. If a complete twist is to be experienced then the body is usually led slowly into position, the speed decreasing as the action reaches its limit and the new base prepared. The release may be quick and explosive if the original base is completely freed, or resolved slowly if contact with the floor is maintained so that weight is taken on both the original and the new base. In the former instance little or no resistance to the unwinding process is possible whereas in the latter the release can be regulated and control over the speed retained. It will be appreciated, however, that these are not the only connections between twisting and time changes, and the more able the performer the more versatile will be his use of speed.

The inherent speeds involved in flight will already have been discovered when dealing with this theme in an elementary way. It is only when sufficient experience and confidence have been acquired, however, that the performer is able to select the appropriate and therefore the most effective blending of speed and energy in order to accomplish a particular objective. Before the more advanced aspects of flight can be attempted the individual should be able to produce and use to good effect the speed gathered in take-off and to control the speed after landing. To revise the earlier work on flight, but now with a time stress, produces an ideal link between the elementary and the advanced aspects of the theme.

Before the advanced theme of gaining, maintaining and terminating balance is introduced, it is most important to have acquired the particular skill involved in controlling the speed of the body. The way of gaining inverted balance for most beginners is to do so with a decrease of speed as the balance point is reached while the reaction to loss of equilibrium is for the body to gain speed. The skilled performer, however, can equally well arrive quickly in a balanced position and check the speed at the precise moment of achieving balance, just as the more able and confident he is the greater the "play" will be when losing balance. A deliberate throwing of oneself off balance and catching the weight again, during floor work, on apparatus or in the air, requires skill, courage and a great deal of self assurance and the more proficient the gymnast the more versatile he will be in lowering himself out of a balance, restraining his body against the pull of gravity.

The effect on most classes of moving quickly and slowly is easily recognisable and the teacher utilises this knowledge both at the beginning and end of a gymnastic lesson. Quick actions enliven, stimulate and animate, which is one requirement at the beginning of a lesson. The consequence of slower movement is to quieten, calm and relax, the aim at the conclusion of a lesson. Although the class will already be used to the different time stress between the introduction and completion of a lesson, when speed has been thoroughly explored a greater awareness and variety should become evident in the selection of preparatory and concluding activities.

If it is the intention to produce skilful and competent gymnasts, then, having first learnt to manage the body in varying situations, mastering the rate at which the body moves should follow logically. This is a facility which must be acquired if the individual is to become expert in the timing of his actions and in the selection of the most expedient use of the skill he has gained.

Teaching

Young children attack physical tasks with great energy and vigour. This is natural, as slow movements require much greater co-ordination and control, which children of this age have not yet acquired. It has also previously been noted that the young are not concerned with restrained actions neither do they need to consider economy of effort. On the whole they are anxious to accomplish tasks in the minimum amount of time. They are, however, content to repeat an action or series of actions many times, but the speed at which they perform rarely alters. Older children and girls, earlier than boys, become interested in slower, more precise and stylish action, although boys at one stage have the greater strength required in order to control the body weight in some of the more difficult slow movements.

With the seven or eight year olds one would not want to inhibit or repress their natural zest and attack in dealing with gymnastic tasks. However, as they become generally more skilful and co-ordinated they can be expected to become increasingly able to cope not only with controlling but also with varying the speed at which they move.

It might be helpful for some children if the extremes were experienced first, and in this case they will involve the individual moving as slowly or as quickly as he can. Each child must be left quite free to choose his own actions if he is to experiment with confidence. The actions selected must be those he feels he is capable of performing safely at the chosen speed.

The general range within the class will be great at first, as each child's interpretation of quick and slow varies. With the help of the teacher and through observation of others, the individual will quickly realise that he is able to extend his own range within the task. Exploring the extremes of speed should not be pursued to any great degree at this stage. Before progressing further the class should be made aware that actions involving flight are necessarily quick, whereas movements leading into a balance position, although not necessarily so, are relatively slower, while other actions can be performed equally well using either speed.

Progression is achieved when the children begin to experience the change from one speed to another and build sequences where a time change is evident. Free choice of action and speed preference should be given but the teacher must check that in each case both quick and slow actions are included. For some children their sequence will consist of all quick movements with perhaps only one slow movement apparent, whereas for others the reverse will be so; some will always place the "odd" action at the beginning or end of the sequence.

When the teacher feels that the class is ready to accept imposed speeds he can begin to dictate the rate at which the class must work and where the time changes are to be placed. The choice of action still remains with the individual. The task may be to:

(a) invent a sequence where the stress is on moving slowly, but the first and last actions are quick, or

(b) compose a sequence, alternate actions being quick and slow.

The next stage could be for the teacher to select a simple action which every child is capable of performing, such as a roll, and to give the following challenges:

(c) choose any roll and repeat it several times bringing about either an increase or decrease in speed;

(d) within a single rolling action bring about a specific time change, e.g. begin quickly losing speed or begin slowly gathering speed.

The class might then be left free to choose other actions and experiment with them in a similar way. It is here the teacher must see that each child selects actions relative to his ability, ensuring that everyone works at his own level. Actions involving inversion, particularly those where weight is taken on the hands, should be included by most. The more skilful the child the greater should be his range of speed, and the more able he should become at performing the same skill quickly and slowly or at the speed necessitated by circumstances. A handstand when performed by a beginner, for example, usually consists of a quick lowering of the upper half of the body and a vigorous upward kick of the legs. The less able the child the less control he can exert over the returning action of the body into the standing position. The more expert performer can complete the action slowly levering the body into and out of the balance position. This requires great strength, much control and co-ordination. Fine timing and judgment in the use of the two extremes of speed are essential before agilities are attempted which involve a quick swing of the legs as in headsprings and shouldersprings.

If a time change within a single action is recognised and the resulting movement repeated a rhythm can easily be appreciated. The child can be made aware of his own individual rhythm and through observation he can also appreciate the different rhythms established by others who may even have chosen an identical action.

Older classes find the more advanced aspects of speed most interesting and a link can easily be established when working with a partner. Just as new timing has to be experienced when working in twos, so rhythms can be copied, not necessarily matching actions but extracting the time pattern and reproducing the essential stresses either within an action or sequence. Further individual work on rhythms can now be explored and accelerating and decelerating rhythms attempted. A sequence of movements can be invented and the intrinsic time stresses appreciated. Climaxes will emerge and natural pauses become obvious and, if the sequence is repeated, a greater clarity can be accomplished and the series of actions logically unified.

If changes of speed are to be employed to advantage,

attention should be drawn to the fine timing involved in the efficient use of springboards and trampettes and in working with mobile apparatus. These skills are dealt with in detail in Chapters 14 and 15.

Not only can children be helped to appreciate that the body is capable of moving at varying speeds but also their attention may be drawn to the economical use of speed when performing any physical task effectively. If children acquire the ability to move at a great variety of speeds and are able to select from this variety purposefully, they are in a position to apply this knowledge and ability not only in the gymnasium but also in related situations where efficiency and economy of effort are required.

Apparatus

Before planning apparatus for work on this theme several principles should be established. The first is that the apparatus itself can do much to dictate the timing of actions. Inclined forms, spring boards, trampettes, swinging ropes and other mobile pieces of apparatus, as well as partners, determine to a large extent a specific use of speed.

The task set is another factor to be considered. If apparatus has to be cleared, a high bar to be reached or a box mounted, then the need for acceleration is obvious and the challenge will only be met if the necessary amount of energy and speed is gathered and used efficiently.

Organisation also has to be re-considered. If the task involves moving slowly, the teacher must provide sufficient apparatus to cover the eventuality of each child spending a comparatively long time on any one piece. Otherwise a situation might arise where one child is working and the rest of the group waiting.

The provision of apparatus to enable a number of children to experiment with changing speed must be prepared with thought and care. If one speed only is to be experienced then a single piece of apparatus will suffice. When asking children to produce a time change, however, a series of actions will probably result. If faced with this task and expected to work on one peice of apparatus such as a horse, buck or box, children are immediately limited either to using the apparatus once or leaving and returning to it. The disadvantages are obvious when considering that there will be perhaps five or six in the group. Long pieces of apparatus such as forms or mattresses which allow for several actions to follow each other easily are preferable. Similarly ropes and bars, which allow three or four to work at once with no hindrance to others, offer greater freedom. A further alternative is to provide a variety of apparatus where children will have sufficient opportunity to move freely, experiencing the full scope of possibilities within the tasks.

It is valuable when beginning apparatus work to give young children the experience of moving consistently at one speed. This stage need not be prolonged but will give the class time to gain confidence in moving quickly and slowly along or over narrow surfaces and at varying levels. The height of apparatus should be kept comparatively low in the first few lessons and, where possible, raised gradually as the children become more experienced. Only single pieces of apparatus are required at this stage and forms, individual or large mats, canes or hoops raised on skittles, steps and bars can be used with the tasks of moving quickly and:

(a) going over or under,
(b) getting on and off,
(c) travelling up, down or along, and
(d) going from side to side.

A possible way of introducing apparatus work on this theme at any age is to give explicit tasks which direct the experience towards the extremes of speed, *e.g.*:

Apparatus—forms.
   Task.—Run and jump off the form, land and work away moving slowly.

These two actions could be repeated travelling the length of the form.

Apparatus—a form used broadways so that three children work at once.
   Task.—Approach and cross the form quickly and return over the form moving slowly.

Apparatus—spring board and mattress.

    Task 1.—Run and jump off the spring board, land and roll over the mat, turn and recross the mat moving slowly. (The teacher can help the class to appreciate that if they return alternately to the right and left, no one need feel hurried by another following too quickly.)

    Task 2.—Run and jump off the spring board, attempt to check the speed immediately on landing and roll slowly across the mat. Own choice of action and speed to return.

Apparatus—bar (hip height).

    Task 1.—Cross over quickly and recross slowly.

    Task 2.—Progress along the bar, getting over slowly and under quickly.

Apparatus—ropes and mats.

    Task 1.—Run and swing on one or two ropes, jump off, land and roll across the mat.

    Task 2.—Progessions would be to include a twist or turn at the end of the swing, necessitating a quick action, and for the swing to be repeated several times,
    or
    added impetus could be gained at the point when the feet are able to contact the floor and recharge the swing,
    or
    the challenge of checking the speed on landing and crossing the mat slowly, could be given.

Apparatus—box top and mats.   Arrows denote possible starting points.

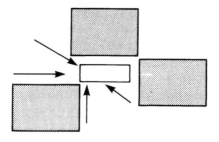

Task.—Approach from any angle, run and jump onto and off or over the box quickly, slowly cross the mat nearest on landing.

The teacher should encourage the children to use the free mats on landing and to follow each other quickly. This will not only enliven their awareness of others but the pace of work will not be interrupted. This challenge can be extended to give the class experience in adapting the speed of their actions with no predetermined ideas, fitting in with others in the group according to circumstances.

The teacher must also ensure that the arrangement includes opportunities for a variety of approach and passing points as shown below.

Apparatus—form inclined to a bar box, and a spring board; form leading up to a horse and mat.

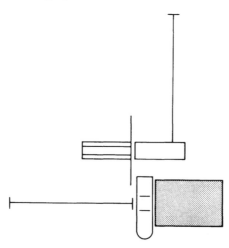

Task.—The whole group to work at the same time, individuals to move over the apparatus, adjusting to others as the situation demands.

This task involves a heightened awareness of others working and requires adaptation both of action and timing, so that a link could be made here with group work—*see* Chapter 15.

Eventually the gradations between the extremes of speed and the natural accelerations and decelerations necessary when using apparatus will become apparent. The class need to be made aware of these possibilities by a careful selection of apparatus as in the following examples.

Apparatus—inclined forms to the lower of two bars, heights approximately 6 and 16.
Task.—Run up a form, pause, turn and run down.

The children should all be able to discover for themselves the natural acceleration and deceleration which occurs in answering this task. They could then alter the action but maintain the increase and decrease in speed, using the top bar to link the accelerating and decelerating actions.

Apparatus—ropes, two bars, height to be fixed according to the ability of the majority of the group.
Task.—Using one to two ropes, swing onto and grip either both or the higher bar. Get off with an increase or decrease of speed.

Apparatus—forms leading up to ropes and mattress. (The distance between the end of each form and the rope can vary according to the ability of individuals and the forms may be altered during the experimental period.)
Task.—Run along a form and leap for a rope, swing and land near to the mat and roll across it.

The necessity for acceleration onto the rope will be obvious but the teacher could help individuals to recognise the possibilities of deceleration in the roll across the mat.

With classes who are working on the advanced aspects of this theme, establishing and repeating a rhythm on apparatus can be both exciting and exacting. Using apparatus such as forms, ropes and bars, a rhythm can be evolved in answer to an explicit action task, such as "get over and under a single bar". With one or two ropes a rhythmical swinging action can easily be achieved or the natural rhythm within a series of actions explored. This sequence could include the use of the floor to approach, an action on the rope, and a means of travelling away from it.

When children have experienced a regular rhythm using one piece of apparatus, they can quickly recognise the possibilities of maintaining this rhythm while accelerating or decelerating using several like pieces. The apparatus selected must either be two or more pieces which are alike or similar, or apparatus with approximately the same dimensions or proportions such as the saddle and horse, the broadside of a form and a box top, or a spring board and trampette.

Most apparatus is adjustable and in the majority of cases the distance between pieces of apparatus can differ and the height at which it is fixed can vary. When introducing accelerating or decelerating rhythms to a class it will probably be most helpful if the first variation of apparatus occurs in height, as for example:

(a) one form, two forms and three forms high (one child will be required to steady the two forms and two to stabilise the three),

(b) one form, a box top and two layers of the box,

(c) a saddle on a low bar, another on a higher bar and the horse,

(d) a beating board or form, a spring board and trampette.

The teacher must ensure that the starting points vary, either beginning with the apparatus which is lowest or the highest, so that not only acceleration but also deceleration is experienced.

Having explored these possibilities the need to increase the distance between apparatus in order to negotiate the increase in height will probably be observed and alterations can be made accordingly.

Some fixed apparatus such as the window ladders, wall bars and ropes, unlike the bars, cannot be adjusted. The ropes, however, are mobile and the size of the swing can vary, therefore an individual could invent a rhythmical sequence and using each rope in turn gradually increase or decrease the amount of speed and energy used.

On window ladders or frames which produce gaps of equal dimensions, rhythmical actions could be performed and repeated, increasing or decreasing speed and travelling up, down, diagonally or across.

It is realised that this aspect of speed uses space and apparatus extravagantly, but if the teacher realises the possibilities he may decide to include perhaps one or two of the above ideas in his general apparatus plan. With an able class who have fully explored accelerating, decelerating and simple rhythms the teacher might feel justified in setting a common task such as, "experiment with accelerating and decelerating rhythms". The apparatus could be selected from the following:

(a) a set of ropes,
(b) window ladders or frame or wall bars,
(c) one form, one box top and two layers of the box, or one form, two layers of the box and a buck,
(d) beating board, spring board and trampette,
(e) two or three bars, if possible, at different heights,
(f) one form, two forms and three forms,
(g) one saddle on the floor, one on a low beam and a horse (if weight is to be taken on the hands on the first saddle, then the teacher must ensure that two children are used to steady the apparatus at either side, but this is not necessary if the apparatus is used for rolling over or sliding through),
(h) a horse, between a saddle on a low bar and one on a higher bar.

A further consideration of this theme occurs when timing and judgment of moving apparatus become necessary. Travelling to make eventual contact with a swinging rope, for example, involves judging the speed of the oncoming rope and timing the action of gripping so finely that no interruption occurs in the process. The following tasks could be given to provide children with such an initial experience.

Apparatus—ropes, trapeze or rings.

    Task.—Hold the rope and swing it away; as it returns, time the moment of contact, grip, and travel on it. (The individual can experiment with contacting the rope at different stages of the swing.)

Apparatus—form and ropes.

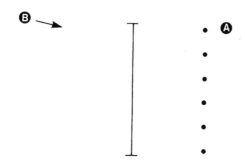

    Task.—In twos—A swings the rope to B—B runs and jumps off the form to swing on the rope and lands on the floor or back on the form. This shows a progression in that a return to the form involves timing in judgment of not only when to grip but also when to release.

Apparatus—two forms and ropes.

    Task.—Set all ropes swinging. Cross and recross from one form to another using each rope in turn and travel along a zig-zag path.

Apparatus—trampette and swinging trapeze.

    Task.—Run and use the trampette to contact and swing on the trapeze. A progression would be to land back on the trampette from the trapeze or to arrive on a piece of apparatus placed on the other side of the trapeze.

An extension of this idea can be incorporated into an aerial circuit where trapeze, rings and ropes can be used in conjunction with trampettes and other pieces of portable apparatus to provide a most challenging arrangement.

Accents and climax within a sequence of actions can readily be recognised and stressed once the class has experienced accelerations, decelerations and rhythms. Appreciation of appropriate actions to stress or highlight can add clarity and enliven the work on apparatus, but the teacher must always be aware of unnecessary or illogical emphasis.

CHAPTER 10

Continuity of Movement in Action

Material

Continuity is a state where movements follow each other in succession, so interwoven that one arises as a natural outcome of the previous action. This does not presuppose that the body must sustain a continuous state of motion. Active pauses which occur as a necessary preparation or involve balance can all be part of an integrated sequence.

In gymnastics skills may be performed as either isolated actions or sequential phrases of movement. The emphasis in the latter is on the ability to combine a variety of actions so fused that the sequence is logically complete. A sequence is a series of bodily actions where recovery and preparation of each action are so skilfully linked and movement so fluent that actual phases are indistinguishable except in variations of rhythm. Economy of effort becomes increasingly important when a number of movements are required. The initial momentum can often be absorbed and utilised in movements which follow and the use of body weight exploited.

All actions are preceded by a preparation and followed by a recovery. The preparatory stage may be brief or comparatively long, the recovery may be quick or take time, and in single actions both can usually be distinguished easily. Within a series, however, it is possible for the recovery and preparation to overlap and it is this blending that brings about continuity.

In gymnastics once movements become deliberate and selected it is not merely a physical preparation and recovery that is considered; mentally the performer has to be alert, anticipating ways of leading logically into the next action.

Those children who are skilled and versatile have a greater choice of action and are therefore more likely to achieve continuity than those who have mastered only one way of leading into and out of a particular skill. Previous work on achieving a variety of preparations for and recoveries from a specific skill proves of added value when continuity has to be considered.

If movements are to be linked smoothly with no irregular interruption occurring within a sequence, the performer must be aware of transitional actions and the part or parts of the body which are about to receive weight. These parts must be prepared in the recovery of the previous action so that on contact with the floor or apparatus the placement affords a sufficiently stable base on to or over which the body may move.

The way in which the body arrives over the base is important. Weight may be transferred onto the new part with a wave-like action involving successive arrival or with the body arriving simultaneously, using an action in which all parts are affected concurrently. Successive arrivals lead more easily to continuous movements; in simultaneous arrivals the action has normally to be recharged before continuing. Reference can be made to other themes, *e.g.* twisting and turning, and loss of balance, where continuity is a natural outcome.

Teaching

Continuity is the thread which runs throughout all other gymnastic themes and is a facet of the work to which teachers should constantly refer.

Beginners find difficulty in linking unlike movements smoothly, although the same action can often be repeated several times. Dissimilar actions which are simple and involve weight transference from feet to feet only, as in running and bouncing, hopping and leaping can be more readily accommodated. A greater skill is demanded when linking actions which include weight transference on to a variety of bases, particularly when inversion takes place and where change of direction and variation of level occur.

A progessive set of tasks for young children could be as follows, each being developed as the teacher deems necessary.

Task 1.—Bounce along using two feet together.

Task 2.—Travel leaping from one foot to the other.

Task 3.—Run and jump, repeat several times.

Task 4.—Transfer weight from feet to hands, repeat this action travelling.

Task 5.—Run and jump, on landing add an action which keeps the body near to the ground.

Task 6.—Start with weight on feet, body tucked, roll in any direction and jump up again. Repeat several times and then change the direction of the roll.

Task 7.—Practice No. 5 with turns in the air.

Task 8.—Take weight on to the hands, get one or both feet high into the air and on landing roll.

Task 9.—Start with weight on feet, body tucked, and roll in any direction. Transfer weight on to hands, back on to feet and end with a jump.

In the early stages the teacher must ensure that the children realise the need to think ahead. This readiness and anticipation should be encouraged and the first steps taken in learning how to land in a position which leads easily into the next movement. This will involve a deliberate selection of part or parts to receive weight and preparation of others required to initiate the following movement. The appropriate speed at which to work could also be considered by older children.

Example.—If a handstand is to be preceded by a forward roll, most children will have to consider how to lead into the inversion. This will usually be by swinging one leg into the air and pushing with the other. At the end of the roll, therefore, the feet should be placed one in front of the other so that they can be used as needed. The speed of the roll must be such that the forward momentum gathered allows the weight to be transferred straight on to the hands without readjustment.

Specific practice could be given at this stage in linking skills:

Task 1.—perform either a forward or backward roll and
  (*a*) walk out of the action,
  (*b*) jump out of the action,
  (*c*) immediately transfer weight on to the hands, getting hips high.

Task 2.—choose an inverted position and
  (*a*) roll out of the inversion,
  (*b*) roll into the inversion,
  (*c*) tip or twist out of the inversion.

At first the stress will be on achieving fluency within a sequence, sustaining continuous movement. The teacher should soon be able to help the class appreciate that pauses are not synonymous with stopping. A change of direction, for example, often requires a hesitation as the point is reached when control of momentum is such that redirection of the body weight becomes possible. Children can experience this quite simply in rocking and rolling on to the feet and bringing about a change of direction.

Once the more advanced situations of working with others have been explored, sequences can be developed to stress continuity. In a partner sequence where each alternately provides and clears the obstacle, the added challenge of linking actions can be a demanding one.

So far continuity has been brought about by a prior selection of actions. The more skilled the individual the more easily he can invent a phrase of movement spontaneously. This, however, involves a facility to recognise and adapt actions relative to each other as they occur. Often Juniors can be observed acting first and then thinking, while older children tend to think first before moving. The spontaneous reaction of Juniors should not be lost and the thought applied to movement at Secondary level must also be encouraged. The ability to "think bodily" should be fostered, as a fusion of action and thought is an important objective in teaching gymnastics.

Apparatus

On apparatus this theme can rarely be taken in isolation

for more than two or three consecutive lessons. It is an underlying consideration in all apparatus work and will often be referred to and drawn upon as a subsidiary idea. For example, once the class, group or individual, has mastered a particular movement challenge, this can then be developed to include continuity of action. If the teacher observes that a class shows a lack of ability of appreciation in this respect, specific tasks can be given to help.

Continuity is, however, a movement idea that could be used successfully to introduce a different way of working to classes who have been used to perfecting isolated skills only, and in this case more time could be devoted to it. Skills already mastered can be included, giving a degree of security, while the added task of joining actions can be readily grasped and easily observed.

In selecting apparatus for continuity tasks the teacher should ensure that the difference between levels is not too great at first. A form leading to a high box, for example, rarely helps the beginner to maintain continuous actions, but a form leading to three layers of the box, or a form inclined on to a bar box, is a more helpful arrangement.

Placing apparatus in a straight line will also facilitate an uninterrupted series of actions, whereas having to manage apparatus placed at right angles tends to hamper all but the most able at first.

Tasks which stress resiliency and where the apparatus is duplicated or is long enough for actions to be repeated, help to ensure that continuity is gained. For example:

1. a form or bar used lengthways,
2. two forms with mats placed between and used broadways,

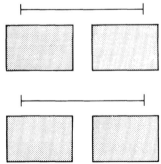

3. a bar with three saddles placed at regular intervals,
4. two low box tops and mats.

Different ways of landing on apparatus can be explored and the teacher could point out that landing on hands and knees on the box top, for example, is a difficult position from which to move with any degree of continuity. If the landing, however, is on to one or both feet, or hands and feet, the next action is comparatively easy to initiate. It is often after arriving on apparatus that adjustment has to be made and the following tasks could be given to help children in this respect. During the experimental period the teacher could refer to successive and simultaneous arrivals on the apparatus.

Apparatus--box (two layers).
  Task 1.—Arrive on the box on one foot, step on to the other and push into a jump, land and roll.
  Task 2.—Run and arrive on hands and feet, make the landing of the feet the preparation to push off again, hands remaining on the box until the feet have landed.
  Task 3.--Arrive on two hands and one foot, use the free leg to initiate the movement off.

Apparatus—ropes and horse or box or buck.
  Task 1.--Use one or two ropes to land on the apparatus. Practise arriving on different body parts, *e.g.* one or two feet, hips, one knee.
  Task 2.--Use the ropes as above, land on one part and from this position use the free parts of the body to initiate the next action.

The ease and fluency with which actions are performed and linked on apparatus are the hallmarks of the advanced gymnast. It is only the most skilled performer who reaches the point where movements merge so naturally that the sequences assumes a logicality and completeness, simple for the observer to appreciate but most difficult to attain.

CHAPTER 11

Partner Work

The aim of partner work in gymnastics is to achieve inter-dependence and this in itself can be challenging, exciting and rewarding. In most situations where two people work together there is a certain amount of "give and take" and this is so in the gymnastic sense. The pair learn, to a greater or lesser degree, to share ideas and select from them appropriately.

Working with a partner involves a high degree of accuracy in performance—an action often has to be repeated exactly, not only in the way that the body is used but also in the timing, and this helps to train movement memory. For example, if one partner is learning an action from the other, the performer has to be consistent in what he does and the observer must be able to understand what he sees. In addition to accurate performance, movement memory and movement observation, other equally important factors have their place in partner work. Working with a partner usually involves experiencing new rhythms and timing. As an individual it is very easy to work on the floor, literally at one's own pace, unless the teacher is aware of this and is able to give specific experience in re-timing bodily actions. When working with another person it is not always possible to use one's habitual timing; it is often necessary to go faster or slower, to accelerate or decelerate in order to match or adapt.

Although all the above aspects of partner work are valuable, the most important factor and the reason for including this type of work in gymnastics, is that in this situation activities can be explored and mastered which are impossible to do alone. The ultimate aim of working with another person in gymnastics is to achieve interdependence.

Material

Unlike other gymnastic themes (with the exception of group work), working with a partner is not so much concerned with a movement idea but with the movement situations arising from two people tackling a common task. It is quite possible to give two children a challenge such as travelling, stressing symmetry and asymmetry and for them to answer with a joint sequence. However, this is of limited value.

The fun and point of working with another is in discovering and mastering the situations that arise from doing, sharing and helping.

There are four basic partner situations.

1. Copying part or whole of a partner's sequence.
2. Making and negotiating obstacles (without contact).
3. Matching actions.
4. Taking all or part of each other's weight.

The above are not arranged in progressive order although copying is probably the easiest and weight-taking the most difficult situation. However, the theme of partner work encompasses so much material that different aspects can be taken with various age groups.

1. COPYING PART OF WHOLE OF A PARTNER'S SEQUENCE

(a) Following pathways.—One travels, the other follows, *i.e.* "follow the leader" relationship. Here it is only the pathway that is dictated by the leader "A": the actual way in which "A" travels—running, leaping, rolling—is not copied. "B" chooses his own movement but follows "A's" track.

(b) Following pathways and copying the main idea.—As above but "B" now tries to copy the way "A" travels. This is not yet exact copying but "B" uses the same idea as "A"; *e.g.* "A" might travel by cartwheeling, while "B" copies the essence of this, *i.e.* travelling with weight on hands, feet overtaking, in a sideways direction.

(c) Copying a short, simple sequence.—In both the above, "A" and "B" have worked simultaneously, or "B" has

followed after a short delay, during which he assesses "A's" movement. Now "A" performs a sequence which "B" observes and then tries to copy. "A's" sequence must be clear in action and remain unchanged in repetition; "B", having observed, aims to perform "A's" sequence as accurately as possible.

2. MAKING AND NEGOTIATING OBSTACLES (WITHOUT CONTACT)

(a) Basic body-shapes forming obstacles.—"A" makes a body shape suggested by the teacher, *e.g.* a curled shape which "B" goes over.

(b) Changing base and angle of approach.—"A" changes the base, *i.e.* takes weight on different parts of the body, but maintains a curled shape. "B" goes over as before but begins to vary the angle of approach.

(c) Changing shape and way of negotiating.—The teacher suggests both the shapes that the obstacle could take, *e.g.* wide or arched, and how "B" negotiates these, *i.e.* under or through.

(d) Choice of negotiation according to shape presented.—"A" selects and makes a body shape which "B" has to negotiate appropriately, *e.g.* by sliding under a low bridge shape; "A" changes his shape and "B" chooses whether to go over, under or through, and how to do this. "B's" choice of action should be relevant to the obstacle make by "A".

(e) Continuous interchanging.—Although each child has worked as "A" and "B" it has been in the nature of having turns at providing the obstacles and taking turns at negotiating. Now it should be possible for "A" and "B" to interchange, *e.g.* "A" makes a shape which "B" goes over, immediately making a different shape for "A".

(f) Interchanging with split-second timing.—As a further development, fine timing could be stressed, *e.g.* "A" rolls into a shoulder stand with legs apart just before "B" goes through this gap and into a movement which leads to a curled position on the floor ready for "A" to leap over.

(g) Moving obstacles.—The most demanding aspect of partners providing obstacles for each other is when the

obstacle itself is moving. In this "A" and "B" would both be moving throughout the sequence, each in turn providing or going over the obstacle.

3. MATCHING ACTIONS

This involves the pair doing exactly the same actions at the same time, or one after the other. The starting positions indicate the possibilities within this idea.

(a) Side by side facing the same direction.—This is probably the simplest way because the starting situation can be maintained throughout the sequence and the performers can see each other whilst working.

(b) Side by side facing different directions.—Here "A" and "B" will work away from, towards or will pass each other and will sometimes be in situations where they are unable to maintain a visual contact.

(c) Facing each other with a mirror-like relationship.—*i.e.* "A" moves to his right, "B" moves to his left.

(d) Facing each other with a non-mirror-like relationship.—*i.e.* "A" moves to his right while "B" moves to his right. This would involve moving towards and away from each other.

(e) Back to back.—This also brings about moving away and towards the partner but because the two cannot see each other the problem of exact timing becomes very difficult.

(f) One behind the other facing the same direction.—The couple can move together and are in a good position to exploit the possibility of moving in canon.

4. TAKING ALL OR PART OF EACH OTHER'S WEIGHT

This can be sub-divided into balance situations, *(a)*, *(c)*, *(d)* and *(g)*, flight situations, *(b)* and *(f)* and lifting situations, *(e)*.

(a) "A" helps "B" to achieve and maintain a balance.—This should be a balance which "B" finds difficult or impossible to do alone.

(b) "B" gets over "A" or pushes off "A" to gain flight.—By means of a brief contact "B" uses "A" to achieve flight;

a well known example of this is leap-frog but there are many other possibilities.

(c) Balancing on a partner.—Having had experience of momentarily taking each other's weight, the children could be introduced to more skilled aspects of working together. "A" selects a position in which he is stable and "B" balances on "A", *i.e.* "B's" weight is taken and held by "A" and "B" is dependent upon "A" to provide a steady base.

The above ways of taking all or part of each other's weight involve one partner acting as a piece of apparatus, solid, firm and unyielding. In the following examples both children are active, continuously concerned with the problems of adjusting and readjusting to each other's weight or timing. This may be seen clearly by comparing *(b)* with *(f)*. In each case "B" achieves flight but in the first situation "A's" role is almost entirely passive, whereas in the second both "A" and "B" are active. There are many ways in which the interdependence of the pair can be developed.

(d) Gaining, holding and terminating balance on a partner. —A progression is when the support "A" is able to adjust his position to help "B" achieve and maintain the balance and then by re-adjustment of his body is able to tip "B" so that at a pre-determined moment balance is lost. Many interesting and difficult balances can be invented once the pair realise that parts of the body can be used to grip.

(e) Lifting, carrying and lowering.—Situations involving one lifting, carrying and lowering the other can be explored and these demand great skill.

(f) Working in twos to achieve flight.—Another skilled aspect of this type of partner work is when "A" helps "B" to achieve flight. "A" may assist "B's" take-off by adding to his ejecting powers, "A" can also help "B" to maintain flight —this would come into the category of assisted flight—and finally "A" can help "B" to make a safe, controlled landing. It is possible, therefore, for "A" to aid "B" in all the three phases of flight or to assist with only one or two.

(g) Counter-balance.—Perhaps the most difficult way in which two people can work together is when movements involving counter-resistance and counter-tension are stressed.

Counter-resistance—By pushing against or "propping up" and making adjustments in the area of their common base and in the angle of leaning, a position is achieved in which both are interdependent, each providing a force which resists and offsets the other. Having established positions of counter-resistance, the pair may then travel, rotate, raise and lower themselves, their actions being towards their point of contact and their common base remaining wide.

Counter-tension—By gripping each other, their common base remaining small, and pulling or leaning away, a balance position is felt when the body is subjected to forces acting in opposite directions, *i.e.* the pull of the partner through the gripping limbs and the pull of the rest of the body, which leans away from both partner and base. A couple can experience many different counter-tensions by using a variety of grips and bases and exploiting the asymmetrical possibilities of the body.

Once positions of counter-balance have been experienced it is profitable for the pair to investigate ways of coming together to achieve them and to discover what happens if, from such positions, one of the pair exerts a stronger force than the other or contact is broken.

Teaching

Before introducing partner work the children should have had considerable experience in managing the body and also be competent in the handling of apparatus. The latter is vital because working with someone else often necessitates handling, gripping, lifting and lowering, and unless previous experience in manoeuvring apparatus is given children cannot be expected to work together safely and profitably. The introductory stages of partner work could be taken with young children and the more demanding work retained until individuals gain in skill and powers of invention.

It is important that the teacher is aware that in introducing partner work he is putting the child in a completely new movement situation. Previously each child has had to consider his classmates in various circumstances. When

working on the floor he has learnt how to change direction or
twist out of the way to avoid collisions, he has moved large
pieces of apparatus with the help of others, and in working
on apparatus he is accustomed to taking his turn and sharing.
Now, for the first time, the stress is not on looking after
oneself or fitting in with a group but on a partnership, on
working wholly with one other person. Because this is a new
situation it is essential that all the introductory stages are
given. With older children it may only be necessary to go
through these simply and briefly in a few lessons, not
stopping to perfect any one aspect but giving them as
situations to be explored. However, with younger children
these stages are invaluable and could be pursued profitably,
the partners working at each problem and perfecting a
finished sequence.

Once partner work involving following a pathway or
copying a series of actions is introduced, the progressions are
varied and depend upon the movement characteristics of the
class. A lively, energetic group, who like to get over things
and are more concerned with what they do rather than how
they do it, would probably enjoy making obstacles for each
other. A class with a fine sense of timing would be more
interested in partner work where exact matching of both
actions and speed is stressed. Having successfully perfected
such sequences, each of these classes could be helped to
improve its bodily skill and understanding of movement by
working at what is, for them, the more difficult aspect of
partner work.

The actual choosing of partners is probably best left to the
children at first, or the teacher can arrange the twos in
approximately the same weight and size, but later, with
growing understanding, skill and confidence, opportunities
should be given for working with different partners.

In giving children experience of partner work it is as well
for the teacher to anticipate certain developments.

Firstly, as soon as a child who hitherto has only worked as
an individual is put into the partner situation a drop in skill
level might result. When this occurs it is because the
attention is not on his own body but directed towards his
partner. However this phase should only last until the child
begins to feel at home in the partnership.

Secondly, many teachers used to the comparative quiet of individuals working become alarmed at the noise that partner work brings. Obviously a "working" noise is desirable and partners will want to discuss their problems. However, the teacher must help the children to realise that too much discussion and planning, particularly at the beginning, results in a re-hash of old ideas, whereas by doing and experimenting new ways are more likely to be discovered. The teacher will also need to be alert to the various partner situations before him, because often with his intervention and help the couple can be encouraged to pursue a worthwhile idea rather than abandon it. Generally, however, the partners will find out for themselves by a process of trial and error which movement possibilities are relevant to the situation.

Thirdly, it must be appreciated that all this takes time. If the children are pressed too soon for finished sequences, the teacher will find the resulting work poor and lacking in invention. Work in twos takes at least twice as long as individual work to arrive at any degree of completion and in any case it is the actual working out of the situation that is of value in the preliminary stages.

Fourthly, it is usual for the first results of partner work to be long, involved sequences. It seems that even though as individuals children have appreciated what is appropriate in their own work, when put into the partner situation they often revert to stringing ideas together with little regard for movement logic. Although they have learnt to select from their own ideas they find this difficult at first with a partner and so nearly everything the pair discover is retained. It is only through doing, observing and discussing that they develop a feel for what is logical and appropriate to the task set.

1. COPYING PART OR WHOLE OF A PARTNER'S SEQUENCE

(a) *Following pathways.*—Here the leader "A" must be helped to realise that it is his track that is important to "B" and so it must be both clear and varied. The direction of the pathway is in relation to the room and will be composed of zigzags, loops, straight lines and circles. The way in which "A" travels (forwards, backwards, sideways) is not copied and is therefore not so important.

(b) Following pathways and copying the main idea. — This is a much more difficult task for "B" and the teacher can help in several ways. Firstly, it is important to see that the space in which the two work is limited otherwise the pathway can become too complicated. If mats are available "A's" track can be confined to approaching, crossing and going round the mat. Secondly, the sequences need to be fairly short, probably not more than three actions. "A" must be encouraged to move with clarity and be able to repeat exactly. Young children would enjoy this task if just one action were repeated, *e.g.* weight on hands and feet alternately on a zigzag track. Older children would be able to recognise and copy more than one action. A typical example would be if "A" ran, jumped, landed and rolled. It would not matter if the take-off was from one or two feet, and neither the position of the body in the air nor the type of roll would be important, "B" would follow "A's" pathway and copy the actions of running, jumping and rolling, *i.e.* travelling on feet, being in the air and finally transferring weight to and from adjacent parts in a rolling action.

(c) Copying a short, simple sequence. —It would be of value here if the teacher gave each child sufficient time to perfect his own sequence of actions. The observer's task is made easier if the sequence he is watching is well executed and consistent. The teacher's role in this partner activity depends to a large extent upon his knowledge of the class. In answering this task many children will find that it is the timing of the copied sequence that is difficult, rather than the actual movements, and it is the teacher who must decide how capable individuals are of achieving an exact copy of both actions and timing. However, it must be stressed that only by constant challenging will individuals widen their movement vocabulary and understanding.

2. MAKING AND NEGOTIATING OBSTACLES (WITHOUT CONTACT)

The point of children making obstacles for each other to go over, under, around and through when apparatus has been specifically designed for the purpose could be queried. This would be valid if a teacher gave this task in isolation and did not develop the idea. When seen within the whole context of partner work, however, making and negotiating obstacles becomes valuable basic training for the more skilled and complex aspects to follow and there is no doubt that children find such situations exciting.

In the elementary task suggested in 2(a), p. 171, the children making and negotiating shapes need considerable awareness and sensitivity towards each other, for jumping over a body presents greater problems than scrambling over a box. The child making the curled shape should appreciate the necessity of keeping his body compact, tucking in all angular parts. The child clearing the obstacle must be aware of the importance of judging exactly where to take off, knowing whether height or length is to be stressed in flight, and landing away from his partner. These considerations are obvious and normally children would take such things literally in their stride, but the teacher should stress them from the safety aspect and because such awareness is vital in the later, more difficult partner situations.

In (b) and (c) the teacher further guides the experience so that the obstacle varies in shape and size and ways of going over, under and through are discovered. The majority of children clearing a small obstacle will run forward and jump over and will want to repeat this several times. Next the teacher could encourage variations: the jump need not always be a forward one, nor from feet to feet; possibilities such as diving over into a roll, cartwheeling over, turning jumps over, rolling under, sliding under, can all be experienced. (See Plates 16—20.)

The teacher, therefore, gives or stimulates ideas in (a), (b) and (c) so that by (d) the children have sufficient material from which to select for themselves. This is an example of the technique of setting explicit tasks which give an experience that can later be the basis for exploratory tasks.

In teaching this aspect it is of value to give partners ample time to work at and perfect a sequence as suggested in (d) and (e). It cannot be said too often that although the teacher may give the class a wide movement experience and encourage variety in ideas, unless the children are given an opportunity to develop these ideas, select appropriately from them and eventually perfect their own sequences, little will be added to their movement vocabulary.

PLATE 16

PLATE 17

PLATE 18

PLATE 19

PLATE 20

The tasks suggested in *(f)* and *(g)* are comparatively difficult but children who are able to accept such challenges will gain much enjoyment and satisfaction from working at these.

It may be necessary with some classes to introduce the idea of coping with a moving obstacle in a simple way first. The following three situations could be given as the starting points upon which each couple would eventually base their own solution to the task set.

Example 1.—"A" maintains a rocking action, "B" assesses the moving obstacle, seeing at what point it is best for him to leap over, and at what intervals this opportunity occurs. Although "A" is providing a moving obstacle his actions are predictable, being repetitive, rhythmic, and traversing the same small area.

Example 2.—"A" repeats a series of compact rolls in a straight pathway, "B" goes over "A" by means of repetitive jumps making a zigzag pathway. The progression here for "B" is that "A" is travelling in one direction, not crossing and recrossing a given area, and therefore as well as getting over "A", "B" must also travel, either in his actual jump or between jumps.

Example 3.—"A" rolls continuously sideways in an elongated position while "B" jumps over "A". Here it is important to note that "B" is faced with two possibilities, either travelling in the same or opposite direction as "A", the latter being the easier. Whether "B" chooses to work towards "A" or travel in the same direction as "A", the actual clearing will demand judgment in the timing and placing of the action.

The teacher will appreciate that when partners are alternately making and negotiating obstacles they are faced with a new situation. In previous work with apparatus, once the pieces have been set up they have not altered in shape or size. In partner work, however, a child can quickly change the shape and outline of his body and vary level, producing a variety of spaces and gaps, so that his partner is constantly having to re-assess the situation confronting him. Similarly, when the obstacle is moving, the challenge is a unique one, none of the conventional apparatus being mobile in this respect.

3. MATCHING ACTIONS

Although it may be necessary for each pair to experience all the different starting situations and their influence on the movements that follow, it will be found that if children working in twos are given the problem of matching their movements in various situations, they will generally include more than one way of working together, *e.g.* a sequence which begins side by side may change, because the children roll backwards along different diagonals, to one of facing each other.

Any task involving the matching of actions and timing is a demanding one. The pair are not only concerned with doing the same action, *e.g.* rolling, but also performing the actions in an identical manner, so that is *what* is done, *how* it is done and *where* are important.

Generally, it will be found that children have little difficulty performing the same actions or series of actions. If the short sequence that the pair is doing consists of an asymmetrical shoulder balance which goes into weight being taken on one knee and then into a forward roll, the average couple will be able to do this side by side or facing each other and achieve a certain degree of uniformity. However, once the pair can do the same actions they should be encouraged to aim for exact matching. In the above sequence they would need to know if the weight is taken completely on one shoulder, how the rest of the body maintains the balance and the way in which balance is ended. The arrival on the knee could be preceded by the whole body tipping or by one leg reaching out towards the floor and the knee gradually taking the weight as it is shifted over from the shoulder. The task of moving identically is a considerable challenge to two children and it demands and encourages a heightened sense of body awareness.

Along with the precision of bodily actions the pair must also consider the timing of these actions. Perhaps one of the pair always rolls slowly, coming naturally to a stop as his feet meet the ground, while the other habitually rushes through his roll, gaining impetus. In order to achieve the same rhythm two possibilities are open to the pair. Either child can abandon his own timing of the roll (not an easy thing to do, particularly with a less skilled performer) and attempt to copy that of his partner, or both could work towards each other's timing, resulting in a new way of rolling for both. The moment the pair achieve a common timing can be one of the most exciting and satisfying results of working together.

Plates 21 and 22 show Primary school girls working on matching partner sequences. In Plate 21 the arrival into the balance has been simultaneous but in Plate 22 the movement after balance has yet to be synchronised as can be seen by the different head positions.

It is in such situations that the "give and take" of partner work is evident and the teacher must see that this is indeed a shared experience and not allow one of the pair to do all the adapting and adjusting while the other continues to work in his own particular way. The degree of "give and take" both in ideas and performance will vary with each couple, and their relative skill and experience must be taken into account, but ideally the work should be the result of joint contribution.

During the working out of a matching sequence the pair will need considerable time to observe each other and to

PLATE 21

PLATE 22

repeat some actions in isolation, but when the whole movement phrase is being perfected it is useful to link the pairs.
One couple watches a nearby couple's sequence and helps
them to achieve complete matching and synchronisation.

4. TAKING ALL OR PART OF EACH OTHER'S WEIGHT

The development here from the three partner situations
described above is that contact is now involved. It cannot be
stressed too strongly that this is advanced gymnastic work.
The teacher is at all times responsible for the safety of the
class and it is dangerous to attempt such tasks unless the
children are already competent and experienced in handling
apparatus. Contact with a partner in order to lift, lower or
balance must never be allowed to degenerate into
uncontrolled heaving and hauling.

(a) "A" helps "B" to achieve and maintain a balance.—
Here the task is for "B" to attempt a balance that he finds
difficult to do alone, with "A" helping in an appropriate
way. If the example of balancing on hands is taken (and in
this partner situation it is likely that the balance attempted
will be an inversion) "A" is free to move and take up any
position in which he will be able to help "B" gain and
maintain balance. Some children will quite happily do a
handstand against a wall but not in a space for fear of
toppling over, so the helpers think that they can give the

security of the wall by catching and holding the legs. This is not only dangerous since the legs are often swung energetically, but usually futile. With a few children who are almost able to do a handstand it may be sufficient for their partners to steady the balance by placing a hand behind the heels.   However, with most children it is the trunk, particularly the hips that need to be helped into the vertical position.   The helper "A", therefore, should be prepared to give support to those parts that need it and gradually to lessen it as "B" becomes more skilled.

When given the appropriate assistance, "B" actually feels what it is like to be balanced on his hands. He is also made aware of parts that he needs to stabilise, *e.g.* shoulders and back, by the points at which "A" is giving him support. In addition, the way in which "A" is helping (holding the hips vertically over the base, stopping the legs going past the point of balance) will indicate where he needs to use more or less energy. If "B" is eventually to be able to take weight and balance upon his hands unaided, "A" must be a sympathetic helper. He must appreciate where and when to give support and how this can be gradually decreased, and through observation he must be able to adjust and adapt his support to "B's" changing needs. If "A" himself has the particular skill that "B" is trying to master, it could be an advantage, but this is not necessarily so.

It should be possible by sympathetic help and guidance from the teacher for children to help each other to acquire balancing skills, although in cases where there is a particular difficulty the teacher may feel that he himself must act as the helper "A".

Problems of balancing the body on bases other than the feet, and particularly in the inverted position, are important in gymnastics and partner work is one way in which the children can become familiar with these situations. Once confidence and mastery have been gained children should normally be able to progress from being helped to working alone on the floor and on apparatus. This, therefore, is an aspect of partner work where the immediate objective is for one to help the other become self-sufficient, although within the context of the partner work theme as a whole it also contributes to the aim of interdependence.

(b) "B" gets over "A" or pushes off "A" to gain flight.—
The brief contact here between the two needs careful
consideration. The child acting as the obstacle must take
up a position with a wide, stable base and be able to resist the
push of his partner as he goes over or around. This means
that "A's" body must be firm and parts such as the shoulders
which might give way under pressure must be stabilised as in
the familiar leap-frog "back" position, by placing the hands
on the knees or thighs. It is also important that "A" knows
from what direction the push will come and where contact
will be made. If "B" is using "A" to achieve flight to the
side or to go around, the pressure will come from that side
at an oblique angle and this will necessitate "A" readjusting
his base.

The point of contact between the two needs attention
because both must realise that certain parts of "A's" body,
e.g. the small of the back, are not able to withstand vigorous
pushing actions, while other areas, such as the hips, can offer
more resistance.

*(c) Balancing on a partner.—*When the pair are able to
cope with temporary contact they are ready to try out
situations in which contact is maintained, and the task of
"B" balancing on "A" is one way of experiencing this. Again
it is necessary for "A's" position to be a stable one with a
base sufficiently wide to be able to withstand the extra
weight of "B", and the problem of choosing suitable parts of
"A's" trunk and limbs upon which to balance has also to be
considered. With "B's" weight being borne entirely by "A"
it is essential that the latter is helped to select positions in
which he can do this safely and effectively, and "B" must
help by keeping a light tension throughout his body, that is,
endeavouring to control his weight rather than becoming a
dead weight draped over "A".

Although this task is ultimately concerned with the
partners balancing upon each other, with some children it
might be a sufficient challenge at first just to bear each
other's weight. Once the feel of the weight-bearing situation
has been experienced, with all the demands it makes upon the
supporter, the couple should be encouraged to lessen the
points of contact until "B" is balancing upon "A".

PLATE 23

PLATE 24   PLATE 25

PLATE 26

PLATE 27

Plates 23 to 27 are of fourth and fifth year Secondary girls balancing on partners. In Plates 23, 24 and 25 the balances developed from maximum to minimum contact as the girls were challenged to free limbs and to rely on fewer supporting parts. In this respect Plates 26 and 27 are particularly interesting, for Plate 26 shows the original solution to the task. This balance was easily gained and most of the time was devoted to adjusting the limbs of the balancer to achieve stillness. However, the suggestion that the supporter should reduce contact with the ground proved to be a much more difficult challenge and the eventual solution is shown in Plate 27.

While it is not essential that the partners in this task are of the same weight and size, the teacher should be aware that the greater the contrast the more difficult the task becomes if each child is to provide the base in turn, and it might be necessary, therefore, to select certain pairings.

(d) Gaining, holding and terminating balance on a partner. —The next step is taken when "A" adjusts his position so that "B" is guided into the balance and, by a further adjustment, causes "B" to lose balance. The stress in this task is not only on balancing but also on ways of gaining and terminating balance with both "A" and "B" actively concerned.

At first the child acting as the base will probably offer flat or slightly rounder surfaces on which his partner balances, but if hands are used to grip various body parts, the possibilities are greatly increased. For example, the use of hands in Plates 23, 24 and 27 should be noted.

(e) Lifting, carrying and lowering. —Tasks concerned with this type of partner work are difficult, particularly when a high standard of performance is demanded. Children need to have a considerable level of skill competence before embarking upon this work and, in addition, the manner in which the partners tackle the tasks together is a crucial safety factor.

In the beginning stages the tasks should be simple and it is advisable to focus attention on lifting and/or lowering in isolation before attempting short sequences involving carrying. Plate 28 is of two Primary school girls who were

PLATE 28

given the task of "Lift your partner into and out of a balance".

It is in the group situation that lifting, carrying and lowering tasks can be fully exploited and therefore further ideas and teaching points are given in Chapter 15.

(f) Working in twos to achieve flight.—Flight is one of the most exhilarating aspects of gymnastics and in partner work it can be achieved by one helping the other. The flight that is gained in this situation should be more than the individual could attain alone, and with the partner's help the actual feeling of flying, of being in the air, is often prolonged.

The three stages of flight, the take-off, moving through the air, and the landing will be dealt with separately for clarity, but the helper, besides being able to assist at any one of these three stages, can also aid at two or even at all three phases.

Take-off.—The aim of the helper "A" is to assist "B's" take-off, that is, he adds his own force to "B's" powers of ejection. If a preparatory run is needed before the take-off, "A" and "B" can already be in contact and as the point of take-off is reached "A" checks, steadies himself and helps "B" into the air. This travelling together occurs when "A" grips "B's" upper limbs and assists the take-off by an upward push at the point of contact. Another possibility would be for "A" to adopt a suitable position in the take-off area so that "B" travels towards "A", makes contact and the ejection is accomplished.

The ways in which "A" can assist the actual take-off vary considerably, an important factor being which part of his body (feet, back or arms) is being used and which area of "B's" body is going to be contacted. The actions of lifting, pushing, pulling and flinging can be used by "A" and although these actions demand a certain degree of strength, the way in which this added energy is given will differ. Lifting implies that "A" retains his contact with "B" and that during the actual lifting the pressure upwards is maintained, while flinging suggests a sudden explosive movement where contact is quickly lost and "B" is thrown or hurled into the air.

In addition to selecting an appropriate action, in order to assist "B's" upward propulsion, "A" must be able to time his help and to apply it in the right direction. If "A" and "B" are travelling together and "B's" take-off is by an energetic thrust from the lower half of the body which sends him upwards and forwards, "A" must time his action of giving impetus to follow on from this. Thus the original ejection from "B" is immediately superseded by that of "A" and the action continued along an upward and forward direction.

Unless "A" is able to judge the force, the timing and the direction of his action correctly in relation to "B's" own take-off, the result will be impaired flight with "B" being thrown off balance, jerked into the air or even attaining less flight than he would achieve alone.

Flight.—The helper "A's" role is again varied. He may keep his hold on "B" during the whole period of flight, resulting in partner-assisted flight. This would involve "A" actually travelling during "B's" flight, pivoting on the spot, or remaining stationary while "B" flies over. It is relevant here to note the difference between carrying a partner and assisting him during flight. In the former the couple remain close together with many parts touching, while in the latter the two are apart with minimal points of contact, so that the partner has an experience of travelling through the air and not one of being lifted off the ground.

The helper also has the possibility of "boosting" "B's" flight *en route*. The example of a couple doing leap-frog action will serve as a useful illustration. If the "back" is sufficiently low for the child going over to place his hands before his feet leave the ground, only a brief period of flight will be gained from pushing against the "back" as he goes over. However, if the latter is comparatively high, the performer will achieve upward flight first from his own take-off and then "boost" this on the way, by pushing against the "back" as he goes over. If the "back" now reacts to "B's" touch not only by resisting the downward push, but also by energetically pushing upward, he adds considerable impetus to "B's" flight.

Landing.—When an individual achieves flight undue preoccupation with making a safe landing often inhibits the actual movement through the air. A child assisting his partner in this way can not only help him to land and recover easily and safely, but also, by relieving him of some of the concern of landing, enable him to appreciate the time spent in the air.

If the helper "A" has held his partner during flight the process of aiding the landing follows logically. "A" will be able to control "B's" momentum, help him to regain a vertical position and also, if necessary, to rebound into one or more resilient jumps.

If "B" has had unassisted flight, "A" must take up a well balanced position and reach towards "B", yielding on meeting to lessen the impact. It must be stressed that "A" is not catching "B" (this is a situation which can be exploited safely and to the full in group work) but is concerned with slowing down his partner's momentum and thereby helping him to control his landing.

If this type of partner work is to be of value the child who is in some way being assisted in flight must himself be able to take-off effectively, land safely and control his body in the air. In fact all the considerations of flight when working individually apply to the partner situation. In addition the performer must be able to gain impetus from his helper by means of a strong, vigorous pushing action, and hold the body with light tension away from the support during assisted flight.

Although the helper "A" must be adaptable, his task is made easier and his help is the more effective if "B" is clear in what he intends to do in all stages of flight. It is important that in repeating the flight sequence the actions retain the same rhythm and timing. The performers should be helped through doing, experimenting, observing and discussing to appreciate *how* "A" helps "B's" jump and *when* he does this.

(g) *Counter-balance.*—This involves complete inter-dependence and so a considerable time is needed by the couple in order to explore the possibilities within the situation thoroughly. Their first task would be to find positions in which they could gain a counter-resistance or counter-tension and in achieving these positions discover how much to yield to and how much to resist each other's weight. In fact at the beginning the pair will not so much attain positions but rather come to jerky, see-saw actions where first one and then the other exerts too strong or too weak a pressure.

However, once this stage has been mastered and the pair know how to adjust to each other, they should be encouraged to experiment with different holds and to find out how to cope with asymmetrical situations. Most couples will begin with a hand or wrist grip because this gives a sense of security, with weight on both feet, either pushing towards each other (counter-resistance) or pulling away (counter-tension). There are other possibilities, for example, a hand can grip the partner's ankle, or the elbows can be used to get a linking grip. When the hold is other than with two hands it becomes possible for the couple to investigate taking weight on other parts of the body, even becoming inverted. They may find it easier to match their positions at first but eventually an interplay between symmetrical and asymmetrical holds, bases and positions should be experienced.

Plates 29 and 30 show very similar positions of counter-resistance. In Plate 29 contact between the pair is made by the soles of the feet and by exerting pressure each maintains the other's position. In Plate 30 another couple has made the counter-resistance more difficult by reducing the point of contact to toes, by widening their common base and by increasing the angle of lean from the vertical.

PLATE 29

PLATE 30

When counter-resistance and counter-tension have been achieved ways of moving can be considered. The previous uncontrolled see-saw action can become a deliberate "to-ing and fro-ing" where first one and then the other partner exerts a greater pushing or pulling action. Travelling together is possible, although this depends upon the ease with which the base can be moved, and changes of level can be brought about.

Although most couples will find the actual holding of counter-resistance and counter-tension challenging there are further progressions for skilled performers. The ways in which the positions are gained can be considered and also what happens when these positions are lost. It is difficult to give general examples here because the possibilities are many. The main aim of the teacher will be to help the children to feel what is a logical way of gaining a particular counter-resistance or counter-tension and then to appreciate the movements which follow once the position has been lost.

Apparatus

Concern for another person in gymnastics is such a new idea for most children that they need considerable time working on the floor during which they can explore thoroughly all the possibilities. To introduce apparatus too soon would complicate matters: the children would not be able to concentrate fully on a partner, the task in hand and the apparatus. It is in such circumstances that accidents could occur. Furthermore, in some instances the partner is used in the beginning stages as an obstacle to be got over or under, and apparatus added to this situation would be superfluous. In the more advanced stages where partners take each other's weight, it is essential that they are given ample time in which to become skilled and thoroughly conversant with the situation. Therefore, no apparatus, other than mats, should be used until the couples are competent and safe in their handling of each other. It is during the floorwork that the teacher helps the children to develop a sense of partnership with real concern for each other, and once this has been attained work on apparatus can be introduced.

With younger children the teacher will probably begin with small apparatus and each couple would have one piece only, *e.g.* a skipping rope, and the task would be explicit. If all the pairs have the same piece of apparatus the teacher will be able to help the whole class generally as well as individuals to answer the task set in a safe and appropriate way.

Once small apparatus and straightforward tasks have been dealt with the progressions are varied but generally it will be a gradual setting of more demanding tasks with more complicated arrangements of apparatus. When planning the apparatus, it must be remembered that it is used to extend a particular partner situation and it should never become so complex that the latter is lost sight of. In the final stages it should be possible for skilled couples to arrange their own apparatus and to set themselves relevant problems.

Apparatus—a skipping rope.

> *Partner situation.*—One child holds one end of the rope, the other end is free.

The rope can be swung round in a circle, the level of which can vary, while the other child uses it as a moving obstacle either going under or over. This child has to appreciate the possibilities of remaining on the spot, moving round in the opposite direction to the rope, and moving with the rope, and the different timing this entails.

> *Partner situation.*—One child holds the rope, the other end is tied. (The railings in the playground, chairs and tables in the hall, and wall bars in the gymnasium can be used.)

If the rope is anchored low to the ground and the other end held high or vice versa, the performer has two spaces in which to work, the angle to the ground giving a range of heights. Short repetitive sequences could be invented, going over and under the rope with the possibilities of travelling up and down. In addition, the holder of the rope himself could become an obstacle so that instead of the performer having a forward and backward path, he could now have a circular track during which he goes over his partner. If the holder grips the rope other than with two hands, *e.g.* holds it under his foot or between his knees, he is able to vary the shape of his body so that his partner has a different obstacle to contend with on each circuit.

Finally the child holding the rope could also have a hoop near him or in his free hand, in which case the following possibilities could be considered.

Apparatus—one or two hoops.

Partner situation.—Two share the apparatus.

The hoop can be placed on the floor and the couple work in a follow-the-leader relationship. In this situation the hoop can be used to get over, by step-like or jumping actions, or with the stress on the area inside and outside, as in hopping in and out. The children need to change from leader to follower frequently and should be encouraged to make their sequences short and repetitive.

"A" could hold the hoop for his partner to get over and through, both from above and below without touching. "A" should experiment with the placing of the hoop; it can be held parallel, at right angles or tilted to the floor and the height can vary considerably. If "B" is given the task of getting through the hoop he has to assess the situation presented by "A" and solve it in his resulting movements. "A" should retain a particular position of the hoop until "B" has found a successful way to answer the challenge and then the two can change roles or "A" can give a further challenge by changing either the height or angle of the hoop or both. This is again a true partner situation: the child holding the hoop is actively involved. He knows the task that has been set and he must realise that it is up to him to place the hoop so that his partner can answer it in a skilled manner. The solving of the problem should not be made too easy or too difficult.

A progression could be that the obstacle, the hoop, is kept moving by "A" so that "B" is faced with a situation that varies. It is important that "A" selects a repetitive action, *e.g.* the hoop can be swung parallel or at right angles to the floor, it can be placed on end and rotated, or it can be raised and lowered. Once "A" has established a rhythm "B" can begin to work. If the task is again to get in and out of the hoop he may need help in judging what is the best point at which to achieve a particular action, *e.g.* jumping in when the hoop is at its lowest, or getting out underneath when it is at its highest.

Further progressions will probably become evident to the teacher whilst taking the preliminary stages. For example, the partner could hold two hoops of the same or different size. They could be placed in similar or different ways either close together or apart, with the possibility of being still or moving.

The teacher must decide at what stage it would be profitable for the children to select actions and perfect sequences. In the latter instance the alternate holding and working, as well as the actual taking and giving up of the hoop, could become an integral part of the final sequence.

Apparatus—mats.
Task.—Work together sharing a mat.

Mats are useful pieces of apparatus in that they give a definite area for work on floor level. The teacher will often find that couples working together do not use floor space wisely, their pathways tending to meander. Mats, therefore, not only provide a definite area for work but, since the floor immediately surrounding the mat can also be used, they can become the focal point of a sequence.

The task of working in a limited area with another person is difficult for some children, and the teacher may decide that when beginning this type of work only a simple challenge is needed. For example, the task could be for the couple to share the mat whilst crossing and recrossing it. This would not involve any matching or copying but the children would need to avoid each other, by changing direction, stopping, going over or under, and precise actions, such as compact rolling, as well as adaptability would result.

Once experience has been gained in sharing a working area, the four main aspects of partner work given at the beginning of this chapter can be considered, and appropriate tasks selected. The following are four relevant examples:

1. COPYING

The task could be to copy a partner's sequence which has been given as an action task to include jumping over the mat, rolling across and going round it with weight taken partly on the hands.

2. OBSTACLES

The mat is used as the focal point of the partner work. The partner making the obstacle could take up his position on the mat, the other working towards him from different angles. This situation is useful when one of the two is rolling under bridge shapes. However, if the couple is stressing flight over the obstacle the landings may be made partly off the mat. In this case, particularly in dive rolling over the obstacle, it would be better for the obstacle to position himself at the side of the mat so that landings would be made wholly on it. Once mats are placed, a certain pathway and angle of approach are suggested, so the teacher must decide which position is appropriate to the needs of each particular couple.

3. MATCHING

Here the couple may be limited entirely to the mat if it is a large one, or to the mat and the space around it. The starting positions, side by side on the mat or opposite each other at the edge of the mat, could be dictated.

4. WEIGHT TAKING

The problem could be one of helping the partner to achieve flight over the mat. The couple would decide whether help should be given at take-off or during flight and positions at the side of or on the mat taken up accordingly. However, as with flight over an obstacle, if the teacher decided that the flight attained by the couple warranted the use of the mat as a landing aid he would re-word the task, getting flight from a distance on to the mat.

Apparatus—a form.

Task.—To work sharing the apparatus.

Forms also provide a focal point for partner work, but they can be used in other ways. When placed on the floor a form gives a change of level, with a wide or narrow surface and a large space above and a small space underneath. In partner work all these opportunities can be exploited. The following are typical tasks each concerned with one of the four basic partner situations.

1. COPYING

A movement task can be given, such as travelling along and across the form showing symmetrical and asymmetrical actions and the resulting sequence may be copied partly or wholly by the partner.

2. OBSTACLES

The form may be considered as an additional obstacle (*e.g.* when selecting pathways which go over the form and under the partner) or as giving added height to the normal partner-obstacle situation. In the latter circumstance it would be possible for three couples to use the form at once with the obstacles on the form and the partners approaching from either side. If a form is available for each couple, a task of starting at opposite ends, working towards each other and passing midway, would probably result in the pair going under and over each other. However, this challenge could also be solved by a swivelling counter-tension in order to change places.

3. MATCHING

If the task is one of matching both actions and pathways the following starting postions could be dictated or suggested by the teacher. An inventive class would readily find their own variations.

4. WEIGHT TAKING

When the form is used narrow side uppermost, partners can work on various aspects of balancing each other, including counter-tension positions. On the broad side of the form all the situations concerned with one helping the other to balance can be repeated, the slightly higher level making this a challenging progression for most children. Flight over or off the form, with the helper standing either at the side of, or on, the form is also a logical progression from the floor work.

Combinations of mats and forms can be used to give variety to the partner situation. Similarly, if forms are hooked at one end on to wall bars, tubular bars, window ladders and bar boxes, or planks hooked on to frames and stools, then additional possibilities of using the variation in height, the slope and the larger space underneath are given.

Although the four main aspects of partner work can still be considered when planning arrangements of *large apparatus*, it is of significance to note that these are not now of equal importance.

1. COPYING

If the couples are still at the stage of copying a part or the whole of each other's sequences and as yet have had no experience of further partner situations, with a few possible exceptions they are not ready for work on large apparatus. The copying situation is usually one of transition from working as an individual to being one of a pair and this can be most profitably explored in floor work or with small apparatus. Furthermore, to put children in the position of having to copy a partner's action on large apparatus could be dangerous and, for many, an impossible task.

However, there are two instances in which it might be worthwhile to give partners the task of copying the essence or the whole of each other's sequence on large apparatus.

With a class inexperienced in the partner situation but able to cope with themselves on apparatus, the teacher could challenge the couples to copy tracks or selected actions. This would be a means of gaining new ideas and serve as a useful introduction to the more demanding partner work.

In addition it is often of value to give skilled, experienced gymnasts such tasks. If the apparatus is arranged as a circuit giving ample opportunities for various tracks, an individual copying another's sequence would probably experience new pathways, actions and rhythms.

When confronted with an arrangement of large pieces of apparatus the partners often start by finding out what each can do. They copy ideas, actions and pathways as a preliminary to answering the task set. However, this is a stage which is passed through quickly and once the pair have explored the possibilities of the apparatus they begin to work in conjunction, with all the "give and take" that this entails.

2. OBSTACLES

This is an aspect of partner work best pursued by most children on the floor or with small apparatus. However, able children would probably find the combination of large apparatus with an obstacle partner work task very challenging. When working on apparatus with more difficult tasks and problems given below most couples will incidentally use their previous experience of going under or over each other. This occurs when their pathways cross or they need to overtake.

3. MATCHING

In selecting apparatus for this type of work the teacher must decide if he is going to:

(a) dictate starting positions and/or pathways,
(b) suggest them by the lay out, or
(c) give couples the opportunity to set their own
    apparatus or pathways or both.

In (a) and (b) all the various possibilities of starting positions and resulting pathways must be considered and catered for. It will be appreciated that certain pieces of apparatus provide ideal opportunities for a couple to work side by side with parallel pathways. Ropes, bars, single or double, with or without saddles, window ladders and wall bars all can be used in this respect with the couple starting side by side and moving forwards, backwards, up and down.

As well as using single pieces in this way, apparatus can be placed to form a continuous straight or angled pathway, thus allowing the two to work from opposite ends or to start one in front of the other with the possibility of overtaking. The following is a selection of apparatus arrangements with tasks related to the main idea of partners matching their movements.

Apparatus—two forms, box and mats.

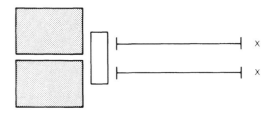

Task.—Start at the points indicated and *either* work parallel to each other *or* the pathways can cross on the box.

Apparatus—two forms and a horse.

Task.—Start at "x", meet on the horse and pass each other to finish in partner's starting position.

Apparatus—buck astride a form.

Task.—Start at opposite ends of the form cross by going over and under the buck.

Apparatus—inclined form to bar box and mat.

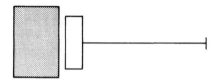

> *Task.*—Both start at the same place, work one behind the other matching simultaneously or in canon, using various pathways.

Apparatus—one buck, two forms and two mats.

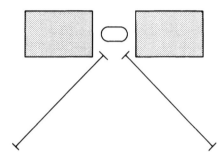

> *Task.*—Own choice of starting position and pathway but at some point both must share the same piece of apparatus.

Apparatus—double bars and two forms.

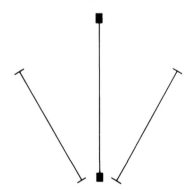

Task.—Use all the pieces of apparatus in a matching sequence. (The bars give the opportunities of matching actions at different levels or working side by side or matching canon.)

Apparatus—ropes, horse (without pommels) and mat.

Task.—Work side by side from ropes to horse and on to mat. (The difficulty here is to time the swing and the arrival.)

Apparatus—double bars and ropes.

Task.—By means of one or two ropes arrive on the bars, use and leave them with matching movements.

The children must be given ample experience of working on teacher-selected arrangements before going on to choose apparatus for themselves and should by then be able to appreciate the different possibilities that individual pieces and combinations can offer.

4. WEIGHT TAKING

Up to this stage the teacher would have given the children specific experience in all aspects of the partner situation by means of carefully selected progressions. Both on the floor and on small apparatus the children will have gained in skill and understanding by working at tasks where one aspect of taking each other's weight has been stressed. It is still possible to work in this way on large apparatus.

Apparatus—two pieces placed apart.

Task.—To help the partner across the gap by assisting his flight in some way.

Apparatus—two pieces, one placed beneath the other, *e.g.* high and low bars, or trapeze and mat or ropes and form. (The distance between the two pieces should not be great.)

Task.—To aid the partner by lifting him from the low piece to the high piece and to help him down by lowering.

Apparatus—a narrow surface, flat or inclined, *e.g.* bars, window ladder away from the wall, bar box or form hooked on to bars.

Task.—To travel along or up the narrow surface together maintaining a counter-tension.

However, it will be found that as larger apparatus and more complex arrangements are used so the couples will select from their past experience appropriate ways of managing each other's weight and not pursue just one aspect. An example of this would be if "A" helped his partner "B" at take-off to arrive on a box. In this position, by means of counter-tension "B" could lift "A" to his level; retaining the counter-tension "A" could now lower "B" to the floor and the latter could assist "A's" landing from a jump off the box. In this particular example assisted take-off, lifting and lowering by use of counter-tension and assisted landing would have taken place.

In the following arrangements of apparatus a problem is presented to the couple, both in the task and the actual set up of the apparatus.

Apparatus—bar at medium level.

Task.—Find and perfect ways of helping each other over and/or on to and off.

Apparatus—three pieces of apparatus of different size and height arranged in a triangle with gaps between.

Task.—To use various ways of assisting each other to cross the gaps.

Apparatus—a high piece of apparatus.

Task.—To find ways of helping each other onto and off the apparatus from above and below.

Work on large apparatus where the partners are continually adjusting to each other's weight is one of the most skilled aspects of gymnastics. Eventually the children should be able to select their own apparatus and set their own problems, but before this stage is reached a high degree of skill in individual body management must have been acquired and all the progressive partner situations experienced.

The organisation of apparatus for partner work needs careful planning. In the early stages each pair may have the same piece of apparatus, *e.g.* a hoop. Later it may be necessary to divide the class, *e.g.* half the couples working on mats the other half on forms. With large apparatus in an average gymnasium it is possible either for each couple to have their own piece, remembering that wall bars and inclined forms can augment the large portable and fixed apparatus, or if long tracks of apparatus have been arranged, for two or three couples to share the same piece.

The teacher should also bear in mind when devising apparatus for other gymnastic themes that it is useful to retain one section at which, as each group arrives, they divide into couples and continue partner work.

The ability to work well with another person is a significant stage of achievement in gymnastics and both the teacher and children should be aware of this. It is essential that the teacher knows the ability of his class before introducing the theme and that he is able to give the children a worthwhile experience. The couples should be led through the progressive stages and aspects of partner work so that they acquire new skills and further their understanding. Only if children have been well taught and have developed mutual care and consideration will they be able to work profitably and safely together and thereby gain in enjoyment, skill and understanding.

CHAPTER 12

Advanced Body Management

In returning to body management themes at an advanced level the intention is to widen the movement experience and to improve bodily skill. This is achieved by *relating* and *developing* aspects of the work previously considered at an elementary and intermediate level. Thus the skills acquired previously are adapted and augmented as progressively more difficult and demanding situations are presented.

A teacher who considers a class capable of tackling and profiting from advanced work probably knows, from his lesson notes and observations, the themes that he wishes to revise and then relate and develop. Therefore, the following material is given in the form of suggestions for advancing gymnastic skill and understanding and enriching a basic vocabulary.

Relating Elementary and Intermediate Body Management Themes

The skilled performer should be able to consider more than one movement aspect at a time and so the themes experienced in relative isolation at earlier stages can now be revised and related. There are many ways of doing this.

EXAMPLE 1.
The aim is to extend the experience and skill of balancing by placing a selected balance within the context of different movement emphases.

If "Choose an inverted balance and hold it" is given as a starting point some children will respond with familiar skills such as headstands, shoulderstands and handstands, although there are other possibilities particularly when the shape of the body is other than elongated and the base is not restricted to like parts. Once the balance has been perfected the following challenges could be given separately and the resulting movement possibilities explored. It may well be found that some challenges are inappropriate to the particular balance selected and then a decision has to be made by the teacher and/or the child concerned whether to adapt the balance to the new challenge or retain the original balance and work on another more appropriate challenge. The final stage would be to produce several phrases or sequences in each of which the original balance is related to different movement emphases.

Task 1.—By rolling forwards and/or backwards get into and out of the balance.

Task 2.—Spring into and out of the balance.

Task 3.—Try to move the base and retain the balance. (This might result in walking on the hands or pivoting on the head and hands or shoulders.)

Task 4.—Experiment with various body shapes—curled, elongated and spread while inverted.

Task 5.—Terminate your balance by twisting and/or turning.

Task 6.—Gain and lose your balance with a symmetrical stress throughout; repeat asymmetrically.

Task 7.—Invent a sequence in which your particular inverted balance is achieved three times. Gain and lose each balance with a different movement emphasis.

EXAMPLE 2

Another way of relating basic ideas would be to emphasise a part of the body and to see how this part is used in various gymnastic situations. For example, legs can be important in actions on the floor and apparatus.

They can—

(a) take the body from place to place as in running and stepping,

(b) lower and raise the body through different levels,

(c) eject and receive the whole weight as in flight,

(d) initiate actions such as twists, turns, loss of balance, *(e)* give the impetus in swivelling and pivoting actions, and to achieve rotational flight,

(f) add momentum to swinging actions on ropes or bars,

(g) support the body, as in gripping a trapeze or bar.

These will not be new actions to most children but by associating actions which have a common idea, movement understanding and skill are furthered. Tasks could be set demanding an emphasis on legs throughout a sequence with at least two different ways of using them included.

EXAMPLE 3

It would also be possible to take one action such as twisting and explore its relation to other movement considerations,

e.g. twisting and changes of direction,
twisting and changes of speed,
twisting in locomotion and stillness,
twisting during flight,
twisting between different levels,
twisting with a partner.

Developing Elementary and Intermediate Body Management Themes

Although a teacher may decide to return to basic gymnastic work for a more detailed exploration there are three themes capable of considerable development at an advanced level. These are weight-bearing, stillness, and locomotion, certain aspects of which result in balance and flight. Both involve much material and are dealt with separately in the following two chapters.

However, it is both possible and profitable for a class to spend a few lessons re-examining some of their earlier movement experiences in the light of increased levels of skill and confidence. In such situations it is essential that the floor work tasks are demanding and that a high level of perfection is expected. In this instance the floor should be considered as offering as much of a challenge as does apparatus.

Apparatus

In the selection of apparatus at this stage the teacher should ensure that it adds considerably to the action or movement task given. Thus the apparatus could be arranged so that a complicated lay-out with considerable variety is presented. However, too much apparatus may result in children just clambering their way around a circuit. Therefore the teacher might select very simple arrangements, working on the principle that less complicated apparatus, as with the floor, can often present the most challenging situations when coupled with a demanding gymnastic task.

The following suggestions are intended to act as guidelines for the teacher who is selecting apparatus and tasks in order to develop advanced body management.

(a) Dissimilar pieces could be used in one arrangement, giving a variety of height, width and surface.

(b) Spaces between pieces could be wide so that flight or assisted flight can take place.

(c) Springboards and trampettes could be used frequently.

(d) Skilled performers could be given apparatus which they arrange themselves in order to answer a specific task.

(e) Individuals and groups can be allowed to select and arrange their own apparatus in order to solve a given problem.

(f) Selected individuals could be encouraged to set their own task on apparatus of their choice.

(g) Mobile situations could be given.

In the latter, where for example, a form is hooked on to a trapeze or between two rope ladders, a completely new situation is presented. To work on apparatus that swings freely at one or both ends could be dangerous, but it is an arrangement in which competent gymnasts can revel and gain considerable satisfaction and enjoyment at an advanced skill level.

Apparatus—medium or high box.

Task.—Arrive on the box by means of a roll. Leave the box by using a forward or backward roll.

This is a progression from the elementary stage where rolling on apparatus is confined to one level or between the floor and low apparatus. Further progressions could be rolling up and down inclined surfaces, and along narrow apparatus, and if a springboard or trampette is added flight can precede the roll on and follow the roll off.

Apparatus—horse with one pommel.

> *Task* 1.—Get on and off asymmetrically.
> *Task* 2.—Arrive on, using the pommel to gain an asymmetrical balance.
> *Task* 3.—Using the pommel, experiment with ways of twisting over and back to the starting position.

Some horses can be raised or lowered at one end so that a slope results. This adds considerably to tasks involving getting on, off and over.

Apparatus—mattress over two forms.

> *Task.*—By rolling, traverse the mattress lengthwise with continuity.

This is a deceptive arrangement, for the bumps and the gap between the forms necessitate compact and elongated rolling in order to achieve any degree of continuity.

Apparatus—low and high bar, with a form inclined to the low bar, a saddle on the top bar, and a box on the far side.

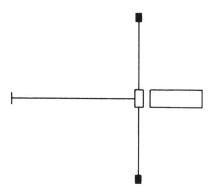

Task.—Use the apparatus to produce symmetrical and asymmetrical actions.

Apparatus—a form inclined to a high bar, trampette and box, one mat.

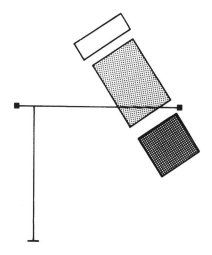

Task.—To produce two tracks, one clockwise, the other anti-clockwise, showing continuity.

Apparatus—a form hooked at one end to a low trapeze, rings or rope ladder. (It may be necessary to tie the form if the hooks appear unstable, and to place a mat under the end of the form to prevent the floor being marked.)

Task 1.—Invent a rhythmical sequence going onto and off the swinging form.

Task 2.—Show ways of getting under and over the moving form.

Task 3.—Experiment with balancing positions while the form is in motion.

Apparatus—two forms arranged in a "V" shape.

Task 1.—Start at A. Select *one* action which incorporates using both forms and the floor between and follow the track indicated, repeat the action negotiating the greater distances encountered to finish at B.

Task 2.—As above but start at B and modify the action to arrive at A.

Subsequent tasks could involve the selection of one constant factor, for example, the action of cartwheeling or a rhythmic phrase, and increasing or decreasing other movement aspects such as body size, level and timing. In most cases, however, the placing of the apparatus itself will dictate changes as long as the same track is followed and the same action repeated.

While in some schools the teacher might consider that working at an advanced body management level is possible for a whole class, in other schools this material might best be explored by option groups or during extra-curricula club activities. For example, the use of mobile apparatus involves safety factors and requires a considerable amount of space. The situations are most suited to those individuals whose interests and ability enable them to profit by the experience in terms of increasing bodily skill and to gain satisfaction from meeting the difficult demands made of them.

CHAPTER 13

Gaining, Maintaining and Terminating Balance

Balancing, the ability to hold the body over a comparatively small base in both motion and stillness, is a fundamental and characteristic gymnastic skill.

The pre-school child is initially concerned with standing, that is acquiring and maintaining an upright position, and then later with walking and running, and all these activities involve the elements of balancing. The young school child is still actively occupied with exploring balancing possibilities. He pares down his base, walking on toes or heels, he deliberately chooses to walk along narrow surfaces and he tries to balance on body parts other than feet.

It is this desire to balance the body both in motion and stillness, together with a high degree of control and skill within the actions, that is exploited in gymnastics.

Material

Although balance is not stressed as such in acquiring elementary body management skills the elements involved in equilibrium should have been explored thoroughly. Thus weight bearing and stillness provide the starting points for work on static balance, where the intention is to hold the body motionless over a small base, and weight transference and locomotion relate to dynamic balance, where the body is moving over minimal supporting parts. Balance is considered here as an advanced theme but the beginnings are established in the basic ways of managing the body.

The act of balancing implies that the body is held over a small base either motionless or while travelling and in biomechanical terms this would be classified as unstable equilibrium. In order to balance the centre of gravity of the body must be above the supporting base or basal area. Various factors affect balance, for example, a heavy body is more stable than a lighter one, a large base facilitates balance more than does a small base and a spread body over the support enables fine adjustments to be made more easily than with a compact or elongated body.

However, the point at which weight bearing becomes balance is not easy to determine since it depends upon the part or parts acting as base and the skill of the performer. It is important that the teacher encourages children to work towards the use of small bases and, particularly, to help children to achieve inverted balances. In addition the teacher's choice of words during lessons on balance is crucial if the movement sensations associated with balancing actions, that is a feeling of perching not resting on a part and of a controlled precariousness, are to be experienced and enjoyed.

In order to clarify balancing actions it is useful to consider the three phases of gaining, maintaining and terminating balance separately. In static balance these phases are easily distinguishable and usually occur once each in turn but in dynamic balance the body moves continuously through the three in succession during the locomotion.

GAINING BALANCE

The ways in which balance is gained vary. In order to achieve an upright balance it is usual for a weight-bearing situation to be assumed and then the base diminished. Inverted balances require an initial action to get the body over the selected base and this is often accomplished by kicking up or swinging the legs. Skilled gymnasts can lever into a balance or arrive in a balance from flight. The degree of speed and energy required to gain a balance depends upon the action and the performer, but there is normally a deceleration and a controlling of energy as the point of balance is reached.

MAINTAINING BALANCE

Once a state of balance has been gained the focus is on keeping it. There is a "point of balance" when the centre of gravity is vertically over the centre of the base. There is also an "area of balance". This is found by shifting the centre of gravity above the base in different directions but always keeping it over the basal area. Thus the range of movement possible while maintaining balance is explored. In static balance it is essential that the "point of balance" is found, while in dynamic balance it is this shifting of the centre of gravity over each successive base that allows locomotion to be achieved during balance.

The shape of the body can vary while a balance is held; curled, elongated, spread and twisted positions all being possible. While balancing small adjusting movements will be taking place all the time, therefore the point made earlier, that a spread position allows greater freedom of movement than does a compact one, is relevant here.

The appropriate tension required to hold the body in balance, particularly during inversion, must be maintained throughout the action. It is inability to sustain this tension for any length of time that can cause loss of balance.

TERMINATING BALANCE

Balance is terminated when the centre of gravity is moved outside the base. For beginners this is synonymous with unintentional loss of control or "going through a balance". Skilled performers can terminate a balance in two ways. Firstly, the balance can be ended by a controlled movement into another position. The centre of gravity is kept over the base until a free body part is placed ready to share the weight bearing. The downward levering action of the legs out of a handstand is an example of this. Secondly, balance can be terminated by a loss of control which would result in a fall if the gymnast were unable to recapture command of his body. Deliberate loss of balance followed by regaining control can be brought about in three ways.

(a) The centre of gravity can be shifted outside the base by tipping the body in any direction, momentum being gained as balance is lost.

(b) The free limbs can execute a strong, quick, whipping action which immediately brings about unbalance.

(c) The base itself can be moved by a vigorous pushing action.

The examples below describe how a balance on hands could be terminated in these three ways.

(a) The legs begin the tilting action which pulls the hips out of line and balance is lost.
(b) The legs part and whip round in a twisting action causing the centre of gravity to shift outside the base.
(c) The arms flex and the hands push against the floor, throwing the body out of balance.

Teaching

In a gymnastic lesson balancing actions of necessity include all three phases of gaining, maintaining and terminating balance. However, recognition of the particular difficulties which will probably be encountered by beginners and unskilled performers is of value to the teacher.

When more than one part constitutes the base these parts are sometimes placed too close or too far apart in relation to the rest of the body. Often there is little awareness of the relation of other parts to the base, the hips particularly being out of line. When the balance is on hands the shoulders need to be stabilised and the adjusting action of the free limbs appreciated. The beginner is rarely able to feel the "point of balance", "the area of balance" and the play between the two. Similarly, when trying to hold a balance there is a tendency to make wild correcting movements which cause loss of balance.

The tensions involved in balance should not be new to the beginner. However, he needs to feel the particular muscular control required to hold each position and in doing so will often err between too much and too little. Inverted balances require an initial forceful action to achieve the upside down position and sometimes there is an inability to hold the body away from the base and collapsing results. Beginners find difficulty in selecting a suitable speed to get into a balance and can rarely control speed as the point of balance is approached.

There will invariably be some children whose failure to hold all but the simple balances is not due to any of these reasons. Fear of being and staying in an unusual position, particularly upside down, and most common of all, fear of toppling over and falling can be most inhibiting. Such children need careful, patient help and their confidence must be built up over many lessons with the teacher guiding each stage rather than forcing the pace.

This raises the question of whether an individual should be helped to experience the "feel" of balancing so that he can eventually perform such skills unaided. The teacher, a partner and apparatus can provide different kinds of "support" and this must be considered as a legitimate means of helping a child to achieve balancing actions.

The teacher should be able to give most help verbally. He may stand by an apprehensive child in order to give confidence, but the need to give physical support should not be ignored. Partner work, where one helps the other to balance, can be invaluable if the situation is sympathetically controlled by the teacher. (*See* Chapter 11 on Partner Work.) The way in which apparatus can be arranged so that balancing is experienced safely is discussed later in this chapter.

Most children can acquire balancing skills if they are led through the progressive stages and are never put into a position of danger. The experience of gaining, holding and terminating a simple shoulder balance can be built upon as more difficult balances are attempted. Growing bodily skill and the resulting increase in confidence would appear to be relevant factors which contribute towards the mastery of difficult balances, particularly those of inversion.

It is vital that the teacher appreciates what constitutes skill in balance. The skilled performer is able to take up, maintain and terminate a balance at will. He can select from a variety of bases, and show versatility in the way he arrives in a balance, for example, from flight or by levering. The gymnast who is confident in his balancing ability does not show the strain of the beginner and his movements to adjust the balance are small and precise.

When confidence in balancing is achieved, playing with the action can be enjoyed. The feeling of instability is not frightening but exhilarating, and the body can be deliberately thrown off balance because control can be regained when necessary. This is also an important safety factor. Accidents often result from loss of balance and falling, and a child who has experienced instability can react to correct the situation.

The poise and the ease with which the expert balances are obvious and his economy of movement and effort the result of accumulated skill. However, the poise and line of the body is not only a gymnastic concern. In gymnastic lessons those children who have recognised what balance entails are in a position to draw upon this experience in other situations.

FLOOR TASKS

Tasks 1—4 are useful as introductions to balance since they recapitulate earlier body management work.

Tasks 5—9 are intended to give basic balance experience.

Tasks 10—11 are concerned with developing balance skills.

Task 1.—Take weight on an area of the trunk. Try to get an much of your body as you can off the floor until you are perched on just a part of your original base.

Task 2.—Take weight on both feet, diminish your base until you are balancing on part of the foot or feet.

Task 3.—Find out which parts of your legs you can use as a base for balancing.

Task 4.—Try to achieve at least a momentary balance on hands.

Task 5.—Experiment with bases composed of two or more parts. (Here the teacher could encourage the use of parts such as the front of the shoulder, forearm and so on.)

Task 6.—Find out what can happen to the rest of your body when you use wide, narrow and pin-point bases upon which to balance.

Task 7.—Gain and hold a balance and change your body shape while maintaining the balance.

Task 8.—Work on a sequence to show at least one static balance and one balance held during locomotion.

Task 9.—Find how many different inverted balances you can hold.

If a teacher can both anticipate the ways in which tasks might be met and, through observation, gain further ideas then it is possible to extend and develop tasks so that the challenges are interesting and progressively add to the children's movement experience.

Reference to Plates 6 and 7 will indicate just how varied and skilled responses to a balance task can be. For example in Plate 6 all the girls have a symmetrical base and for all but one this is on two hands. However, the variety in the shape of the body above the base is interesting; all except one are symmetrical but within this elongating, tucking, arching and spreading can be seen. The girl on the mat can only maintain her balance momentarily but she has placed her hands appropriately and her body shape is clear. In Plate 7 the placement of hands is interesting and in contrast to Plate 6 four girls have their hips low and close to their base although the variety of spreading, tucking and elongating is still evident.

The actions preceding and following a balance must be considered as soon as the basic idea has been understood, therefore tasks should be given requiring balances in a phrase or sequence of movement.

Task 10.—Select one balance; find various ways of moving into it and out of it.

Task 11.—Try to gain inverted balances with bases consisting of unlike parts, such as hand and forearm. Select two or more, and invent a sequence where the loss of one balance leads into another balance.

As children become adept at static balancing, less movement occurs and the teacher must avoid a slowing down of the lesson pace. It could be relevant here to refer to and recall the previous experience of locomotion and to work on dynamic balance though this is most profitably explored on apparatus.

Apparatus

The use of apparatus in balance considerably widens the scope of the work. Apparatus that is inclined, narrow, slippery, high, moving and at different levels provides balancing problems not encountered at floor level. All parts of the body cannot act as a base on the floor but bar-like apparatus enables the front of the hips to be used and in this situation body parts can be below the base, which is impossible in floor work. At ground level the base has to be flat or nearly so but when using the pommels, ropes, bars, trapeze, rings, wall bars and the narrow side of forms, the supporting parts can grip.

The value of apparatus as a means of helping children to feel a balance position such as inversion has been mentioned. This point is worth the teacher's consideration. Many children will not balance upside down on the floor but will try to do so with a support or something to grip. This enables them to experience the orientation involved in inversion and yet feel safe while doing so.

Balance is included in partner work when one helps the other to balance and when counter-balancing situations occur. (*See* Chapter 11 for balance in partner work.) When arranging apparatus the teacher may decide to have one group working in twos on mats with these ideas.

It must be stressed that balancing on apparatus demands a skilled use of the body. A few of the tasks suggested could be tackled profitably by beginners as part of their basic gymnastic experience but the majority of the tasks are for children who already possess a certain degree of competence and skill.

Primary and Middle

Younger children are interested in balancing while moving on apparatus and this should be catered for. Older children can tackle specific balancing tasks, some may be able to arrive on apparatus in a balance, and most will be able to balance when on apparatus and get off by terminating balance.

Apparatus—individual mats, mats and mattresses.

> *Task* 1.—Cross the mat showing dynamic balance and finish holding a balance.
>
> *Task* 2.—Balance at the side of the mat, cross it and finish in a balance at the other side.

Apparatus—stilts.

> *Tasks.*—In the playground a group can use stilts at various heights to practise balance walking. When this has been achieved variations in direction can be tried together with turning and pivoting actions.

Apparatus—two forms, narrow side uppermost and placed parallel, close together.

Tasks.—Tasks concerning balance walking as well as using hands and feet can be given. (Height has been added to the balance situation but since the forms are used together the problem of placing the supports in a straight line is omitted.)

Apparatus—form, narrow side uppermost.

Tasks.—This apparatus gives opportunities for balance walking with height; the added difficulty is to place the supports along a straight line on a narrow surface. The introductory tasks involving travelling on hands and feet, as well as feet only, could be supplemented with travelling in different directions and changing direction, once a certain degree of proficiency is achieved. Working backwards along such apparatus takes time and queues might arise so it may be expedient to combine such apparatus with one or two mats for practising static balances.

Apparatus—two or more   parallel horizontally suspended ropes across the gymnasium or hall.

Tasks.—Horizontal ropes can be used for balance walking and travelling on hands and feet, the movement of the ropes being an extra consideration.

Apparatus—high horizontal ladders, poles and planks.

Tasks.—This type of apparatus is ideal for dynamic balancing activities. The narrow surface and the height require courage and give a sense of daring.

Apparatus—inclined slippery planks or forms.

Tasks.—Such apparatus allows for sliding and balancing activities to be combined. The body is balanced over the selected base while the sliding movement takes place and in these actions both static and dynamic balance is experienced.

Apparatus—low stools, box tops, steps, stage blocks.

> *Task* 1.—Balance on the apparatus, use a free part to lead you on to the floor.
> *Task* 2.—Get onto and off the apparatus and at one point hold a balance.
> *Task* 3.—Balance upside down at the side of the apparatus, lower your legs and place them on the apparatus, get on and jump off.

Apparatus—boxes, stools, or stage blocks at hip height.

> *Task* 1.—Start and finish away from the apparatus. Get on and off achieving one balance on the apparatus and one on the floor.
> *Task* 2.—Lie on the apparatus, place your hands on the floor and with the apparatus as a support take weight and balance on your hands.
> *Task* 3.—Arrive on the apparatus feet first, hands to touch the floor first in coming off; include at least one balance.

Middle and Secondary

The following tasks require considerable skill, some being only for advanced performers. If the teacher has assessed the ability of his class correctly there should be little danger in attempting such tasks.

Apparatus—mats.

> *Task* 1.—Experiment with inverted balances—choose one and find how you can achieve and lose it.
> *Task* 2.—Roll and/or rock into and out of a balance.

Apparatus—forms.

> *Task* 1.—Balance using the sides or top of the form. (*See* Plate 31.)
> *Task* 2.—Use the floor and/or the form to gain an inverted balance. (*See* Plate 32.)

PLATE 31

PLATE 32

Apparatus—form narrow side uppermost.

> *Task* 1.—Travel along the form balancing on different parts of the body.
>
> *Task* 2.—Travel across the form achieving a balance on the form.

Apparatus—low inclined forms.

> *Task* 1.—Travel down the form holding at least two balances.
>
> *Task* 2.—Travel on a zigzag pathway up the form using the two levels for balancing.

Apparatus—bars, hip height.

> *Task* 1.—Balance on the hips with or without hands gripping. Experiment with ways of getting into and out of one balance.
>
> *Task* 2.—Balance on the hips, place hands on the floor and with the bar as a support hold an inverted balance. Gradually lessen the support.
>
> *Task* 3.—Arrive poised on the bar. Travel along the bar using the floor as necessary and include two other held balances.

Apparatus—two bars, low and high.

> *Task* 1.—Balance on the top bar, resolve the balance to arrive on the low bar and balance there.
>
> *Task* 2.—Experiment with balances using a divided base between the floor and the low bar or between the two bars.

Apparatus—box top, or mattress over a form, or low bar.

> *Task.*—Balance on the apparatus using parts of the lower half of the body as a base, tip to lose balance, land and roll.
>
> When working on terminating balance the apparatus must be very low if the original base is provided by the hips or part of the legs. This is because when the body is tipped, it is the hands, arms and shoulders which receive the weight and do so from height might result in injury. Conversely, when the balance is on the upper half of the body the apparatus should be high. This allows the tipping action to be prolonged and there is sufficient space for the body to regain the upright position and land safely on the feet. As skill increases the apparatus in each case can be raised or lowered.

Apparatus—box, horse or buck, full height.

> *Task.*—Balance on hands on the apparatus, tip and land feet first on the mat.

Apparatus—two ropes.

Tasks.—Tasks resulting in inverted balances where the hands grip the ropes help to give the orientation experience mentioned earlier. In addition ropes can be used to pull the body out of balance and to provide a challenging situation for balance when used in conjunction with the floor.

Apparatus—box, horse or buck, hip height.

Tasks.—Such apparatus can also be used to give support to inverted balances. The performer starts on the apparatus and places the hands on the floor near to the apparatus. The weight is then shifted gradually on to the hands with the apparatus providing support at hip level. Progressions would involve the gradual lessening of the support and eventually the apparatus could be used to push from to gain balance.

Apparatus—swinging apparatus such as ropes, trapeze, rings and rope ladders.

Tasks.—This apparatus can be used in conjunction with balancing tasks. The problems of balance are increased considerably when the apparatus is moving.

Apparatus—box, three or four layers.

Task.—Jump on to the box and hold your arrival, get off by gaining and terminating an inverted balance.

Apparatus—ropes to box.

Task.—Swing to arrive in a balanced position on the box, get off with weight on hands.

Apparatus—ropes to bar or narrow form.

Task.—Swing to land poised on the narrow piece of apparatus, tip off and roll. One progression which follows arriving in a balance from a swing, is to arrive in a balance from flight (*see* Chapter 14 on Flight.)

Apparatus—high bar, high box and a low box, three mats.

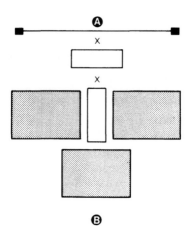

Task 1.—Achieve a balance on each piece of apparatus within a sequence.

Task 2.—Travel from A to B showing a balance on each level.

Task 3.—Choose your own pathway but your sequence must include divided balances at the points marked "X".

Apparatus—two forms, a buck and a mat.

Task 1.—Travel using *both* forms including at least two held balances. An inverted balance is to be used to get off the buck.

Task 2.—Balance on the forms and tip off to each side in turn. Slide over the buck into an inverted balance on the mat.

Apparatus—horse, springboard, and a box top placed on a mattress.

Task.—Arrive on the horse balanced with weight on hands, achieve a balance with a divided base on the mattress and box.   Aim for continuity between the balances.

CHAPTER 14

The Body in Flight

Flight occurs when the body moves unsupported through the air. Jumping is a natural action, particularly of the young: children jump for joy and through excitement, accentuating the upward, or they jump when thwarted and frustrated, stressing the downward part of the action. There is a basic desire to overcome gravity and being in the air gives a sense of freedom.

Flight can be considered as a form of locomotion when the stress is on travelling through the air, or as a way of transferring weight when the stress is on the part or parts used for take-off and landing. In advanced flight the actions of the body whilst airborne are more important. Being in the air is a unique situation and in gymnastics flight is exploited and developed to a high degree, giving the work one of its essential characteristics.

Material

In considering flight three phases become apparent—the take-off, the actual flight and the landing.

TAKE-OFF

The aim is to get the body into the air and to do this gravity has to be overcome. The legs are the main ejectors and although other parts can be used it is the lower half of the body which, by virtue of its construction, is most efficient in projecting the body into the air.

The action of the body at take off can be likened to a series of hinges and springs which are compressed and then released. The take-off considered here is from the feet but the principles are the same whatever part is used. Ankles, knees and hips flex and by thrusting against the floor or apparatus eject the body into the air. The flexing is comparatively slow, in preparation for the main action. The extension is executed quickly, resulting in a vigorous, explosive effort. The change from flexion into extension is vital in any take-off. Small jumps may require only a partial flexion of ankles, knees and hips large jumps necessitate the full use of the ejecting mechanism. The preparation is always downward and the thrust upward, but both the preparation and the thrust may be modified according to the desired direction of flight and the intended action of the body in the air. The upper part of the body joins in the downward flexing action and the chest, particularly the "centre of levity" becomes important in the upward thrust.

FLIGHT

Flight, which begins as soon as the body has left the ground, can be subdivided into linear flight, in which the body is vertical, and angular flight, which involves rotation. In linear flight the great outburst of energy required at take-off should be partially dissolved, otherwise the body is strained and the freedom of being airborne lost. Throughout such flight a slight tension should be maintained in the whole body, particularly in the head and upper parts, so that there is a sense of moving easily through the air. The skilled performer can experience a moment of suspension when the body appears to hover between the upward surge and the downward drop.

If the take-off for linear flight has been effective the whole body is likely to be stretched. This extended position is needed on landing and so can be held throughout flight, but there are other possibilities. The shape of the body can be altered by tucking, spreading and arching, while the possibilities of symmetrical and asymmetrical positions are virtually unlimited provided that all these actions are initiated at take-off.

The direction and trajectory of linear flight can vary. The ususal direction is forward but flight backward, sideways and diagonally is possible although any linear flight with too great a horizontal component at take-off needs a subsequent action if rotation is to be checked and the vertical position maintained. The pathway through the air can be one where distance gained or height achieved is emphasised, with variations between.

In angular flight rotation occurs and this incorporates all forms of turning up to and including the 360° somersault. Turning in the air can take place about any one of the three axes and the resulting actions can be seen as the direct counterparts of the rolling, wheeling and "walking-over" activities which involve contact with the floor. It is also possible to rotate simultaneously about more than one axis; a twisting somersault being composed of turning about the up-down and side-to-side axes.

LANDING

Although it is possible to land on various parts of the body, the feet usually perform this function and in order to achieve safe landings certain actions are essential. Technically the landing begins as contact between body and floor is made but there must be a preparation for this moment while the body is still in the air. The preparation consists of an extension towards the landing area so that on contact the body can yield easily, acting as a shock absorber. (*See* Plate 33.)

PLATE 33

The way in which the landing is effected will depend upon what the body has been doing during flight. If linear flight stressing height has been achieved the action on landing will consist of the body "giving" downwards over the base. If the linear flight has gained horizontal distance then the impetus of the body as it lands will cause an immediate transference of weight continuing in the same direction. Such landings are also necessary as a safety measure when turning has taken place during flight. When a small area of the body is the first part to make contact, as in a one foot landing, injury could result unless the weight is transferred immediately onto the other foot and the action taken into running or onto other parts resulting in rolling.

Since the landing action is similar to the flexion prior to take-off, the capacity of the body to be resilient can be exploited and another jump or a series of jumps achieved. This means that the slight tension achieved during flight is not dispersed on landing but recharged during the brief contact with the floor. Circumstances are sometimes such that to rebound or roll from a landing is not possible. In a restricted situation where a partner, a wall or apparatus limits the space available, the checking of momentum in a safe way is vital. The flexion on landing has to be followed by a deliberate straightening of the body to gain the stability of the vertical position.

Teaching

Flight should occur in most gymnastic lessons whatever the main movement idea. The exhilaration of flight is not gained immediately; to some the feeling of being unsupported in the air is frightening. The teacher, therefore, has a great responsibility. Children can never enjoy gymnastics if they are uneasy in the air, and in such situations the safety of individuals is in doubt..

The elementary stages of flight (*see* Chapter 5), where bouncing and other activities involving resiliency are stressed, serve a dual purpose. They give the basic experience of leaving and meeting the floor, as well as fostering confidence. As take-offs and landings become more proficient, so the period of flight is increased and only classes well trained in the basic work will be able to exploit the situation.

Advanced flight could be taken with experienced Middle school and older children as they reach what might be termed the "flight readiness" stage. When this theme is introduced it would be valuable to review some of the earlier resiliency tasks, for although the stress will be on actions in the air, the longer the flight the more important the preparation and recovery.

BODY SHAPE DURING FLIGHT

This can be developed from earlier work where parts of the body are emphasised while in the air but in this situation the whole body is involved in gaining and holding the shape.

The previous experience of moving symmetrically and asymmetrically can be recalled and now investigated in the air. A double take-off will probably lead to a symmetrical shape and a single take-off to a shape with a one-sided stress. It could be an added challenge to achieve asymmetrical flight from a double take-off and vice versa. When experimenting it will be discovered that a double take-off usually sends the body vertically upwards while a single take-off leads to horizontal flight. In the latter situation the use of the free leg could be stressed to gain a swinging impetus at take-off or to anticipate the shape to be held.

The teaching points to consider are:

(a) that the whole body participates in the shape, particularly the head, which is often misdirected towards the landing area,

(b) that the shape is held clearly without strain for as long as possible,

(c) that the take-off and landing are not impaired because of the focus on flight.

"OFF-BALANCE" FLIGHT

The position of the body in linear flight is normally vertical or nearly so. This gives a sense of balance and stability despite the loss of contact with the ground. In angular flight the body is often tipped or tilted without gaining full rotation. This is usually termed "off-balance" flight because the action is similar to that on the floor when a balance position is lost and a sensation of lability experienced.

"Off-balance" flight demands the confidence to throw the body into a diagonal direction and the ability to land safely. Inevitably the landings are in the nature of a fall and a quick adjustment and transference of weight are needed if injury is to be avoided and control regained. This work is obviously for those possessing great skill and can be taken profitably and safely only with classes whose movement experience is considerable. In schools where gymnastic clubs exist as part of extra-curricular activities, off-balance flight would provide ideal material for able individuals.

Tipping the body while in the air can be achieved only when the flight is prolonged, therefore apparatus which assists take-off and can be used to fly onto is most useful when this theme is explored. Such apparatus is discussed later in this chapter.

TURNING IN FLIGHT

When a shape is held during flight there is a feeling of pausing or hovering in the air. Turning in the air gives a sense of carrying on the action instead of arresting it.

Turning around the vertical axis during flight is mastered quickly by all children. Quarter, half and three-quarter turns bring about a change of front and are used extensively in floorwork. The run-up is usually forward and at take-off a pivoting action occurs. The arms, and in a one foot take-off the free leg, can add a swinging impetus to the pivot. Young children often throw themselves upward and around from a standing start. Here the upper part of the body prepares by twisting away from the direction of the turn. It is the explosive release of the twist together with the push of the legs that sends the body up and into a turn. Children should be encouraged to turn to both left and right and to discover how a single take-off influences the direction of the turn.

After a turn around the vertical axis, the landing is usually on one or both feet. In a single foot landing the body continues to rotate after the landing foot has touched the ground and this foot must be released quickly otherwise ankle and knee are liable to be twisted. Weight could be transferred on to the other foot and then into a series of steps where the turning is continued and allowed to peter out. In landing on two feet, as from a forward run and a half turn, the act of turning facilitates weight transference and a backward roll frequently follows.

Turning around the side-to-side axis in flight demands considerable skill. If the starting position is on the feet a half-turn in the forwards direction on to hands brings about "catspring-like" actions and dive rolls. The teacher will find that these skills and variations of them are within the capabilities of most children. In the beginning stages the hands may be placed before the feet leave the ground thus obviating flight. Although this might be accepted at first the teacher should encourage flight with the idea of springing up and over on to the hands. The teaching points here are that the hands yield on impact, the head is tucked and the back rounded so that a roll results. Some children may be able to flex the arms on landing and use a pushing action to send the body backwards through the air to land on the feet again.

In addition to forward and backward half turns from feet to hands the upper parts of the body can act as the base and flight can occur forwards and backwards onto feet. Recognisable skills such as headsprings and shouldersprings would come into this category. Some individuals will be able to fly from feet to hands and onto feet continuing in one direction, as in handsprings. Variations can be produced by having a one-sided stress and, in repetitive actions, bringing about a climax.

Complete turning in flight about the side-to-side axis results in forward and backward somersaults. These can be part of floor work but generally apparatus is used to assist the take-off and prolong the flight. Once forward and backward somersaults have been achieved they can be combined with twisting and arching.

Turning around the forward and backward axis during flight brings about cartwheeling in the air. This is another example of an action during flight which has its counterpart on the floor. Children capable of such work can be encouraged to use each side of the body and to combine this with twisting. Plates 34—37 show various aspects of turning in flight.

Turning in flight requires considerable skill and when introducing children to this work the teacher's role is much more specific than in teaching the elementary aspects of the

PLATE 34

PLATE 35

PLATE 36

PLATE 37

theme of flight. Saftey precautions and bio-mechanical considerations mean that teaching is no longer a matter of providing relevant open ended situations to be explored but becomes the presentation of carefully guided and explicitly structured stages. Furthermore, since individual help is often needed the advanced stages of angular flight might best be taken as an extra-curricular activity. However, although the thematic material is considered advanced, in that children need a high level of skill before attempting such work, it is an area of gymnastics which has considerable appeal for young children. Such children often have the appropriate body build, weight, spring and confidence which allows them to revel in aerial experience and at this age this aspect of gymnastics would appear to be particularly relevant to their interests.

Apparatus

Apparatus, a partner or a group can assist an individual at one or more of the three flight phases. Partner- and group-assisted flight are discussed in Chapters 11 and 15.

APPARATUS ASSISTING TAKE-OFF

If the natural spring of the child has been cultivated during the early gymnastic themes the teacher will find that there is an easy transition to apparatus. However, unless the basic work has been taught well such apparatus cannot be used effectively. The teacher should realise that springboards and the like are not to be used as a substitute for the performer's own ejecting powers, but as a means of gaining additional impetus at take-off.

The various types of apparatus used to assist take-off can be considered progressively. A form or box top gives a raised "step up" start, as does an inclined plank or storming board where a run usually precedes the take-off. This type of apparatus does not aid take-off by its construction but by the way it is placed and used. Simple arrangements of such apparatus could provide the link between unassisted take-offs and the use of springboards.

Beating boards give only a little assistance but the many kinds of springboards and twinsprings give considerable impetus when used well and, when this apparatus is introduced, it is vital that the children are given time to explore its potential. This means that the springboard should be used first in isolation and not given immediately as a means of getting on to a high piece of apparatus. In this situation the teacher should ensure that the area of the springboard giving maximum assistance is used and that children are encouraged to master both single and double take-offs. The teaching points are that the stress is on going up out of and not down into the springboard. In addition the body should be in line with the upward thrust gained, so that whether using one or both feet the body must be over the base at take-off.

When using trampettes the introductory stages are particularly important, especially with trampettes where the bed is at an angle to the floor. Since the trampette is used sloping towards the performer there is a danger that the novice will be thrown backwards in flight. Although springboards are best used first without any other apparatus, when starting work on trampettes, it is expedient to use an aid that will keep the weight forward.

The following is suggested as one way of introducing take-offs from trampettes.

(a) The performer sits or kneels on the trampette and bounces, getting the feel of the "give" and recoil of the bed.

(b) Small, standing jumps are experienced with a partner who stands in front or to the side of the trampette, holding hands or forearms. After five or six jumps the performer *steps* off.

(c) Following a few repetitive bounces the performer jumps off, the partner keeping contact and assisting the landing.

(d) A hanging rope which touches the front of the trampette or a bar at chest level could be used as the support instead of a partner.

(e) The first free take-off should have a short approach walk, later a run, with only a slight output of energy and always be on to a rope or bar, which should ensure that the weight is brought forward.

As confidence is gained so full use of the trampette will result. The teaching points are that the approach is controlled, that the centre of the bed is used and that as the body begins the upward movement there is a lessening of tension resulting in a lightly held position or action.

When efficient use of springboards and trampettes has been achieved, movement ideas which have been explored at ground level can be re-introduced.

(a) Symmetrical and asymmetrical take-offs and flight.
(b) Changes of level, direction and speed occur when using springboards and trampettes and may therefore be stressed.

APPARATUS THAT ASSISTS FLIGHT

Although in gymnastics flight occurs when the body moves unsupported through the air, hanging apparatus and pieces upon which swinging can take place give a sense of being airborne when used well, and so can be considered as assisting flight. Usually the apparatus is gripped by the hands and the body suspended, although other parts can be used on the trapeze and rings. Some children grip easily and can hold themselves away from the apparatus, others hang and have no sensation of moving through the air. This is particularly so of heavily built children. In such situations the teacher should set progressive tasks that give opportunities for practising gripping and holding.

Apparatus—ropes.

Task.—Jump on to the rope, try to get your head and shoulders above your grip then lower yourself to the ground.

Apparatus—ropes, form and mat.

Task 1.—Stand on the form, grip the rope, push off, swing and return to the form.
Task 2.—Stand on the form, grip and swing on the rope to land on the mat.
Task 3.—Start away from the apparatus, run and, using the form to gain height, jump onto the rope, swing and land on the mat.

Apparatus—ropes and two forms.

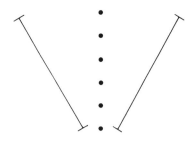

Task 1.—Swing from one form to land on the other. (The forms are placed so that the children can challenge themselves by selecting a distance relative to their ability.)

Task 2.—Develop a rhythmic sequence using two or more ropes in turn.

Apparatus—ropes and trampette.

Task.—Use the trampette to get high on to a rope, swing and drop off. (Here free flight precedes and follows the assisted flight.)

Once children can swing easily they enjoy making their own tracks around apparatus arranged as the circuit below, where ropes provide the means of getting from one piece to another.

Apparatus—a set of ropes, or rings and trapeze, wall bars, inclined form, horse, form narrow side up and box.

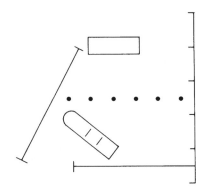

Bars, particularly the cylindrical type, can be used to fly onto and off; the flight can often be boosted by building up the swing on the bar.

APPARATUS ASSISTING LANDING

When great height has been achieved the landing is usually on to mats or mattresses which partially absorb the shock of landing. However, such apparatus cannot give much assistance and it is still necessary for the performer to use his full landing technique. Trampettes can be used for an intermediate landing and in this instance the slope is placed either towards or away from the performer. The jumps will be down from high apparatus and on to the trampette, which will immediately send the body up into the air again and the second landing can be on the floor or another piece of apparatus. In this situation the body does not "give" on contacting the trampette as it would when landing on a firm surface. The ankles flex, but there is only a slight movement of knees and hips, the body being comparatively taut so that the thrust gained from the trampette is transmitted effectively.

FLIGHT TASKS ON APPARATUS

The teacher should bear several important points in mind when selecting apparatus for flight tasks. Mere height of apparatus does not give a feeling of flight. If a task involving jumping off a high box is given too soon, although some children will go upwards many will drop, having a sensation of falling, not flying. In this situation it would be better to have a low box with a task of jumping on and off and gradually build up flight experience.

Some pieces have obvious flight associations. It is easy to jump onto and off a box but difficult to jump over lengthways. A horizontal bar is often jumped over but it needs great skill to jump and land on such a narrow surface. High apparatus, bars, rings and trapeze encourage jumping upwards, while the placing of mats often dictates or influences where the landings will be made. As well as giving opportunities for flight upwards and downwards the teacher should consider flight from one piece of apparatus to another. In the latter instance the apparatus should be broad and, if possible, placed so that each child is able to select the distance he is to cover. It is important, too, that landings from flight are made on to apparatus which is stable and will neither tip nor slide away.

A teacher who has brought his class to the point where flight can be considered with apparatus will not need suggestions for arrangements and tasks, however, the following examples are given to indicate the ways in which flight can be related to other themes.

Apparatus—ropes, form, mattress.

> *Task.*—Assisted flight on to the form, off on to the mattress and return to catch the swinging rope arriving back at the start. (Assisted flight, continuity and timing.)

Apparatus—springboard placed at the corner of a box, mats.

> *Task.*—Weight on hands to get on to the box, spring off showing a clear shape, land resiliently. (Flight and body shape.)

Apparatus—springboard to two boxes of the same height placed lengthways and parallel.

> *Task.*—Flight into weight on hands, either going through the gap, legs over or under, or over one box. (Flight with twisting and turning.)

Apparatus—ropes, trapeze and rings.

> *Task.*—A swinging sequence showing twisting on one piece and turning between two pieces. (Assisted flight with twisting and turning.)

Apparatus—trampette to bar or horse or box.

> *Task* 1.—From flight arrive on apparatus poised and balanced. Balances to be inverted symmetrical or asymmetrical. (Flight into balance.)

> *Task* 2.—Flight over the apparatus with or without contact. This task could be augmented by

> > (*a*) stressing symmetrical or asymmetrical use of the body;
> > (*b*) limiting the weight bearing to one or both hands;
> > (*c*) dictating the pathway of the body; over, through or to the side of the hand or hands.

Plate 38 shows flight onto a rope from a trampette placed a considerable distance away.

Plate 39 shows the last flight phase in a task involving flying onto and off apparatus with turning.

PLATE 38

PLATE 39

It must be stressed that because flight is a vital part of gymnastics it needs to be taught well. Experience and confidence should be built up over the years so that when advanced work is tackled the children are able to enjoy flight and to work safely.

CHAPTER 15

Group Work

This is a progression from partner work, a group being composed of three or more. In gymnastic group work the aim is to explore the possibilities of working with and adapting to others of the same or different abilities and movement preferences in order to achieve group inter-dependence. The gymnastic group is a working unit held together by a common aim.

Material

It is useful to consider the material for group work under three headings:

1. Basic partner situations which can be adapted to the group situation.
2. Basic partner situations which can be fully exploited and developed by a group.
3. Group situations.

1. BASIC PARTNER/GROUP SITUATIONS

Of the four basic partner situations discussed in Chapter 11, three can be readily adapted to the group situation.

(a) *Copying part or whole of a sequence:* this can be tackled by a small group each individual in turn acting as leader. The progressions from copying pathways to copying short sequences are all possible but most profitable with a group of three.

(b) *Making and negotiating obstacles without contact:* one can provide an obstacle for the rest of the group to negotiate in turn. Two or more of the group can combine to make one obstacle or provide two or more separate obstacles.

(c) *Matching actions:* in a threesome such challenges can be met by all moving together. In groups of four or more the matching is usually achieved in canon.

2. BASIC PARTNER SITUATIONS DEVELOPED BY A GROUP

The basic partner situation of taking all or part of a person's weight can be developed considerably by a group.

Balancing.—One can balance on two. In the early stages the two should be at the same level; later, the child who is balancing can be presented with two different levels. When a static balance has been achieved, the two supporters can help the performer into the balance position, tip him off balance and help him to recover afterwards. A group of four or more would be able to produce many variations of balancing on each other including pyramid-type formations. However, whereas in partner work most balances are likely to be static, in group work it is possible for dynamic balances to be explored fully.

Lifting, carrying and lowering.—This is a situation to be exploited in group work. One child can only bear his partner's weight for a short time but within a group one person can be lifted and carried a considerable distance before being lowered. It is important that the carrying should have some objective. The aim could be to carry a child from one piece of apparatus to another, help him on to a high piece of apparatus, or lift him from an inversion, change his position during the carrying and place him upright on the floor.

Flight.—As one person can help another in all stages of flight so can a group help one of its number. Here again the help should be considerable compared with the partner situation, and prolonged flight as well as catching (instead of assisted landing) could develop. In addition a small group can work on assisting some or all of the phases in both linear and angular flight.

Counter-balance.—Three, or at the most four, children can work together on counter-resistance and counter-tension which in this situation is usually associated with lifting and lowering.

3. GROUP SITUATIONS

These situations can be considered as either movement stressed or apparatus stressed.

(a) *Movement stress:* although it is invaluable for individuals and partners to explore aspects of movement themes such as rhythm and climax (speed) and pattern (space) a new dimension can be added to these through group work. Groups of three to six can explore fully the possibility of rhythms where the numbers allow for repetition, accent and extended phrasing. Similarly small and large groups can work on group patterns where aspects of body shape are developed into group shapes.

(b) *Apparatus stress:* the group can exploit apparatus, particularly moving apparatus, in ways which are either impossible for individuals and partners or can be achieved only in a limited manner. Apparatus tasks for groups are given in the section on apparatus with a particular sub-section on moving apparatus.

Teaching

Group work is regarded as an advanced theme but, as with partner work, it consists of several aspects, some of which are very suitable for experienced Middle and Junior school children. Plate 40 shows three Junior school girls working at a matching sequence involving static balances. It is interesting to note that although they have synchronised their timing the balance has yet to be fully matched. In Plate 41 another threesome is shown in the middle of a matching and patterning sequence. The group of four children in Plate 42 has combined matching and obstacle work but has yet to perfect timing.

There is no doubt that when children have acquired a certain degree of skill they enjoy working with others and gain much satisfaction from the results. However, in this work skill and satisfaction will come only when the children feel safe in the group situation. Confidence and safety stem from the mastery of the body and movement understanding. Situations in which children work together and are

PLATE 40

PLATE 41 *(above)*   PLATE 42 *(below)*

responsible for each other must be introduced carefully and the teacher should see that all the precautions given under partner work are taken.

It is in situations involving lifting, carrying and lowering that the teacher should be particularly careful to ensure that the groups are working skilfully and safely. In order to avoid strain the children lifting must be able to work efficiently as a group. This entails keeping the child to be lifted close, getting under him, pushing upwards and using the strength of which the lower half of the body is capable. Furthermore, they need to hold him in such a way that his weight is evenly distributed or balanced about the point of gripping or holding. The child being lifted also has a vital part to play in such activities; if sufficient introductory work has been given he should be able to hold himself easily and resiliently and in addition be alert and ready to adapt to the changing situation.

The actual carrying will mean, firstly, that the supporters must be in a position from which locomotion can take place and, secondly, that in moving they must not be in danger of losing their hold. During the carrying the supporters may actually change their grip or alter the situation of the one being carried, particularly if in lowering they are placing him on to a body part different from that when the lifting started.

The lowering process is similar to the lifting one and again great care is needed to ensure that it is done safely and efficiently. When the one being lowered has regained contact with the ground, the supporters must maintain their hold and continue to bear part of the weight, relinquishing it only when they feel that he is in a position to assume complete control. The child being lowered must prepare the part or parts that are going to receive his weight, otherwise injury might result, particularly if the supporters give up weight bearing too quickly. If weight is to be taken on the hands these need to reach out towards the ground and yield on contact; the amount of "give" will depend on whether the weight will stay on the hands or be successively transferred to other parts of the body.

The size of the group influences the way in which it acts. This is an important factor when the teacher is deciding how to divide a class and what challenges to set. Three children will work together much as in the partner situation, occasionally dividing into two, who match or support, and one, who is lifted or ejected. A foursome will either work as a matching group or split into two interchangeable pairs. A group of five will only occasionally work identically; they will tend to split into a two and a three, or four will help one, as in carrying or catching after flight. A group of six will usually divide into three couples or two threesomes, changing between these. Groups of more than six are unwieldy, and the most profitable group work seems to come from units of three, four or five.

Since children working in groups will have had considerable gymnastic experience the teacher will find that his role changes as the work progresses. At the introductory stage he may need to set specific tasks, offer suggestions and help groups to see how certain situations could be developed. Very soon, however, the groups will become self-sufficient. They challenge themeselves, have many ideas from which to select and are generally independent. At this stage the teacher is more of an adviser, helping the group to clarify ideas, seeing that there is a give and take and not allowing one child always to dictate. Although leaders, in the sense that they are the most forthcoming in ideas, will emerge, it is interesting to note that these are not necessarily skilled performers but children of varying abilities.

As in partner work, the teacher can anticipate certain developments during the exploratory stages of group work. These are: an initial deterioration of an individual's movement, much discussion, the need for a long working time and the tendency to string together ideas or contrive situations. However, these stages should be passed through quickly and if the children have been well taught the teacher will see in their final group sequences the fusion of much of their previous work together with new skills and further movement understanding.

Apparatus

The group situation is most fully explored on apparatus. To introduce the idea the teacher could give each group a variety of apparatus, well spaced, and set tasks which involve an awareness of others working.

Apparatus—double bars, wall bars, two forms, box and three mats to form a large circuit.

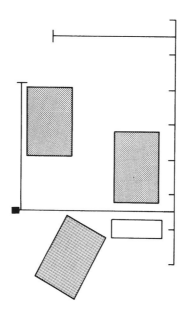

Task 1.—Group of 3 to 6.
All start at different points on the apparatus. Choose your own circuit and by adjusting your actions, speed and direction, avoid others.

Task 2.—Group of 3 to 6.
Work as before, but instead of taking avoiding action when your pathways cross, go over or under each other. (Moving obstacles.)

For progression fewer pieces of apparatus could be used with less space and a specific group task given. Apparatus and tasks can be set which combine some of the situations given under 1, 2 or 3 of the section on material on page 247.

Apparatus—ropes and bars.

    Task.—Group of 3 to 6.
        Matching actions to arrive on and leave the bars, either
        simultaneously or in canon. (Matching, timing, rhythm.)

Apparatus—window ladder or hinged frame.

    Task.—Group of 3 to 6.
        Matching actions to ascend and descend. This would
        result in a pattern-stressed sequence. (Matching, timing,
        patterning.)

Apparatus—box or horse.

    Task.—Group of 3.
        Get on, off and over, singly and together. (Rhythm,
        timing.)

Apparatus—horse over form.

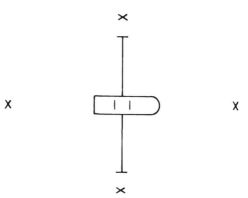

    Task.—Group of 4.
        Start at the points indicated and work towards the
        horse, passing each other by going over and under.
        (Rhythm, obstacles.)

Apparatus—bar box or buck.

    Task.—Group of 3.
        Arrive on and leave by means of counter-tension,
        lifting or lowering.

Apparatus—low box or buck.

> Task.—Group of 3.
> Each one in turn to be helped over the apparatus by assisted flight.

Apparatus—trampette surrounded by mats.

> Task.—Group of 3 or 4.
> Invent a rhythmical sequence of jumps on to and off the trampette.

When groups have perfected sequences on teacher-selected arrangements they will be ready to choose their own apparatus and/or to set their own tasks.

GROUP WORK ON APPARATUS THAT MOVES OR IS MOVED

The various types of swinging apparatus can provide challenging situations for both small and large groups when, for example, tasks involving timing or rhythm are given. In such circumstances individuals can set the apparatus in motion for each other so that fine timing and judgment are involved.

It is also possible to augment the normal swinging apparatus by fastening small apparatus such as a hoop between ropes, form inclined to a trapeze and so on. These arrangements need to be checked carefully before use to ensure that the apparatus will remain secure in use, that the floor will not be marked and that no pieces are subjected to stresses greater than those for which they were designed. With unorthodox arrangements of swinging apparatus tasks involving different kinds of balance and flight during the group sequence can present particularly demanding problems.

It is an added challenge if a group is given static apparatus which has to be manipulated during the sequence. The purpose of moving the apparatus is that the change of situation presents new opportunities for working.

> (a) Apparatus can be used in one situation, moved as part of the sequence and then used in its new situation, e.g. a form could be used normally and then inverted

and work resumed, or its placement altered by inclining it to the wall bars.

(b) The apparatus could be held in its new situation by some of the group whilst the rest work on it, *e.g.* a form could be held away from the ground and used as an obstacle to get over, with or without contact.

(c) The apparatus could be used by one child while the rest of the group move it, *e.g.* a form or box top can be lifted or tilted while one person maintains a balance on it.

The moving of any apparatus should be an integral part of the group's sequence and although the number in each group will determine the size and weight of the apparatus that can be manipulated easily it is often the smaller pieces such as saddles and trapeze bars that can be used most profitably.

Group work with mobile apparatus is undoubtedly exciting to children provided that they have the necessary degree of skill and inventiveness to work in situations requiring a high level of co-operation.

CHAPTER 16

Scheme of Work

This book deals with gymnastics in Junior, Middle and Secondary schools, however, it is also of interest to look briefly at what children might be doing in Nursery and Infant classes.

In Nursery schools and reception classes children can be presented with a variety of movement experiences ranging from large, whole body movements, as when climbing, swinging, running or jumping, to the comparatively controlled actions required in manoeuvring in, out and through quite small spaces. This scrambling over apparatus is not yet gymnastics, in the sense in which it is used in this book, but rather movement play. Nevertheless, some Nursery children and certainly the majority of Infants may well respond positively to suggestions made by the teacher aimed at widening their movement vocabulary whether these be in the form of questions or made as observations.

The characteristics of Junior and Middle school children — their liveliness and boundless energy, their love of daring and sense of adventure along with the enthusiasm with which they set about learning new skills — have led an increasing number of physical educationists to regard this as the "age of gymnastics". Their build too is such that weight and height in relation to strength make certain gymnastic activities comparatively easy to accomplish. Reasons of a different nature are given in Chapter 2 which support the notion that it is in these schools that a place for gymnastics in education can best be justified.

Some children between the ages of thirteen and fourteen who have been taught well for six or seven years may reach a stage, physically, where further work becomes repetitive.

Others may well have matured beyond the point where inversion, flight and fall can sustain their interest. In both instances it would seem reasonable to allow such individuals the right to opt out of further gymnastic lessons. There will be a minority, however, who prefer gymnastics to other forms of physical activity and they should be given the opportunity to master advanced skills. This might best be achieved if such pupils either continue gymnastics as an extra-curricular activity or join a local gymnastic club.

There may also be a case for including gymnastics in the Secondary school for those eleven-, twelve- and thirteen-year-olds whose previous experience has been neglected or limited and for these children the teacher should select material appropriate to their needs and interests. But for those teenagers who reach Secondary High schools at fourteen or thereabouts with little previous gymnastic experience it is highly debatable whether they should be introduced to this activity in a class situation. In such cases it might well have to be accepted that, unfortunately, an opportunity has been lost, although this is no more of a loss (and some might consider it less) than an individual whose artistic or linguistic development, for example, has been impaired by lack of early experience.

In the situations outlined above certain problems have to be met and however these are resolved by the teachers concerned the criteria applied in reaching solutions must be first and foremost educationally justifiable. (*See* Chapter 2.)

The plan on p.259 is meant to be used as a guide and is an outline based on the equivalent of one gymnastic lesson a week over a period of seven years. Although a suggested progression is given as to when specific gymnastic themes might be introduced, the length of time spent on each and the link between past and present work must finally be left to the discretion of the teacher. A chronological division has been used as a basis but it is appreciated that this is only one factor to be considered in the development of the work. Many such variables can contribute to the standard and rate of progress in any one school; a member of a Junior school staff, for example, may happen to be both a knowledgeable and enthusiastic gymnastic teacher, the Headteacher himself may be particularly keen, or there may be a gymnastic club

PLAN

	JUNIOR			SECONDARY		
7–8 years	**8–9 years**	**9–10 years**	**10–11 years**	**11–12 years**	**12–13 years**	**13–14 years**
Locomotion, Stillness, Weight bearing } Elementary Body Management	Weight bearing, Weight transference } Elementary body management, Control of body weight	Stretching and curling, Twisting and turning, Control of tension } Intermediate body management	Symmetry, Asymmetry } Intermediate body management	Advanced flight	Body shape—Space	Advanced body management
Pathways, Direction } space	Direction, Level } Space, Quick, Slow } Speed	Acceleration, Deceleration } Speed, Continuity	Balance, Control of tension, Flight, Control of energy, Continuity	Advanced balance	Rhythm, Climax } Speed	Mobile apparatus
		Partner Work: (1) Following pathways (2) Copying (3) Obstacles	Partner Work: (4) Matching (5) Moving obstacles	Rhythm, Climax } Speed	Partner Work: (7) Lifting and lowering (8) Counter-balance counter-tension	Group work
				Partner Work: (6) Taking all or part of partner's weight	Group work	
				Work in threes		

organised in the immediate vicinity out of school hours. Junior and Middle school teachers will also realise that if classes of nine- or ten-year-olds have received competent teaching over a period of several years and adequate opportunity to work on suitable apparatus, then some of the more advanced work should be undertaken.   Often the ability of older Juniors is underestimated and this despite the young Olympic champions whose level of gymnastic competence demonstrates so obviously the skill potential of this age group.

Surely then it is of crucial importance to recognise that, as far as gymnastics is concerned, the monopoly of the Secondary school in terms of fully equipped gymnasia and specialist teachers is becoming increasingly difficult to justify and if the educational needs of younger children are to be acknowledged and fully realised then resources must be re-directed in favour of Primary and Middle schools.

Bibliography

Allen, J. *Sense and Sensitivity in Gymnastics: a Teacher's Guide to Educational Gymnastics.* Lond: Heinemann. 1969

Allison, J. *Advanced Gymnastics for Women.* Lond: Stanley Paul. 1963

Anderson, M. *Inventive Movement. Physical Education in Primary Schools.* Lond: Chambers. 1970

Bilbrough, A. and Jones, P. *Physical Education in the Primary School.* Lond: University of London. 1963

Briggs, M. *Movement Education. The Place of Movement in Physical Education.* Plymouth: Macdonald & Evans. 1974

Brooke, J.D. and Whiting, H.T.A. *Human movement—a Field of Study.* Lond: Kimpton. 1973

Buckland, D. *Gymnastics.* Lond: Heinemann. 1969

Cameron, W. and Cameron, M. *Education in Movement in the Infant School.* Oxford: Blackwell. 1969

Cameron, W. and Pleasance, P. *Education in Movement, School Gymnastics.* Oxford: Blackwell. 1963; second edition 1965

Cope, J. *Discovery Methods in Physical Education.* Lond: Nelson. 1967

D.E.S. *Movement: Physical Education in the Primary Years.* Lond: H.M.S.O. 1972

Holbrook, J. *Gymnastics: a Movement Activity for Children Aged 5 − 11 years.* Plymouth: Macdonald & Evans. 1973

I.L.E.A. *Movement Education for Infants.* Lond: I.L.E.A. 1966

Learmouth, J. and Whitaker, K. *Movement in Practice.* Huddersfield: Schofield & Sims. 1976

Lewis, B.J. *Gymnastics.* Conference Report: Focus on Gymnastics. A.P.W.C.P.E. 1978

L.C.C. *Educational Gymnastics. A Guide for Teachers.* Lond: L.C.C. 1962; second edition I.L.E.A. 1965

Mauldon, E. and Layson, J. *Teaching Gymnastics.* Plymouth: Macdonald & Evans. 1965

Ministry of Education. *Moving and Growing. Physical Education in the Primary School. Part One.* Lond: H.M.S.O. 1952

Ministry of Education. *Planning the Programme. Physical Education in the Primary School. Part Two.* Lond: H.M.S.O. 1953

Morison, R. *Educational Gymnastics.* Lond: P.E.A. 1956

Morison, R. *Educational Gymnastics for Secondary Schools.* Lond: P.E.A. 1960

Morison, R. *A Movement Approach to Educational Gymnastics.* Lond: Dent. 1969

Munrow, A.D. *Pure and Applied Gymnastics.* Lond: Arnold. 1955; second edition 1963

Pallett, D. *Modern Educational Gymnastics.* Lond: Pergamon. 1965

Prestidge, P. *Women's gymnastics for Performers and Coach.* Lond: Faber. 1972

Randall, M. *Basic Movement. A New Approach to Gymnastics.* Lond: Bell. 1961

S.E.D. *Physical Education in Secondary Schools. Curriculum Paper 12.* Edinburgh: H.M.S.O. 1972.

Stuart, N. *Competitive Gymnastics.* Lond: Stanley Paul. 1964

Webb, I. *Women's Physical Education in Great Brtain 1800–1966 with special reference to Teacher Training.* M.Ed. thesis. University of Leicester. 1967

Williams, J. *Themes for Educational Gymnastics.* Lond: Lepus. 1974

Williams, J. *Skill in Gymnastics.* Conference Report: Focus on Gymnastics. A.P.W.C.P.E. 1978

Williams, J. *The Importance of Gymnastics for Individual Development.* Conference Report: Focus on Gymnastics. A.P.W.C.P.E. 1978

Index